Antonia Clare • JJ Wilson

Speakout

Intermediate
Flexi Students' Book 1

with DVD-ROM and MyEnglishLab

2ND
EDITION

Pearson Education Limited
Edinburgh Gate
Harlow
Essex CM20 2JE
England
and Associated Companies throughout the world.

www.pearsonelt.com

© Pearson Education Limited 2015

The right of Antonia Clare and JJ Wilson to be identified as authors of this Work has been asserted by them in accordance with the Copyright, Designs and Patents Act 1988.

First published 2015
Seventh impression 2019
This edition published 2016
ISBN: 978-1-292-16096-2

Set in Aptifer sans 10/12 pt
Printed in Slovakia by Neografia

Acknowledgements
The Publisher and authors would like to thank the following people and institutions for their feedback and comments during the development of the material:
Australia: Erica Lederman; **Hungary:** Eszter Timár; **Mexico:** Hortensia Camacho Barco; **Poland:** Konrad Dejko; **Spain:** Sam Lanchbury, Victoria O'Dea; **UK:** Lilian Del Gaudio Maciel, Joelle Finck, Niva Gunasegaran.

Text acknowledgements
We are grateful to the following for permission to reproduce copyright material:
Extract on page 25 from "Fraud Fugitive in Facebook Trap", 14/10/2009, http://news.bbc.co.uk/1/hi/world/americas/8306032.stm, copyright © BBC Worldwide Limited; Extracts on pages 37, 70, 161 from *Longman Active Study Dictionary*, 5th edition, Pearson Education Ltd, copyright © Pearson Education Limited, 2010; Extract on page 44 from "Millionaires prefer Gap to Gucci" 05/10/2003, http://www.bbc.co.uk/print/pressoffice/pressreleases/stories/2003/10_october/05/mind_millionaire.shtml, copyright © BBC Worldwide Limited; Extract on pages 44-45 from "Have you Got What it Takes to be Millionaire ?", *The Telegraph*, 05/06/2014 (Shirley Conran), copyright © Telegraph Media Group Limited; Extract on page 80 adapted from 'The secret of success' interview with Malcolm Gladwell, BBC Focus, Issue 197, 01/12/2008, p.23. Presenters Jenny Osman & Ian, copyright © Immediate Media Company Bristol Ltd; Extract on page 105 from "12 Giant leaps for mankind" by Rob Attar, *BBC History Magazine*, Vol.10, no.7, pp.42-47, copyright © Immediate Media Company Bristol Ltd; Extract on pages 116-117 adapted from "I am the Ethical Man" by 22/02/2006 and "We are all ethical men and women now" 13/04/2007 by Justin Rowlatt, http://news.bbc.co.uk/1/hi/programmes/newsnight/4736228.stm, http://www.bbc.co.uk/blogs/newsnight/2007/04/we_are_all_ethical_men_and_women_now.html, copyright © BBC Worldwide Limited; and Extract on page 121 adapted from "Top Ten New Restaurants in East London", *Traveller*, 09/05/2013, source: http://www.cntraveller.com/recommended/food/top-10-new-restaurants-east-london/viewall. Reproduced with permission from Conde Nast.

Illustration acknowledgements
Fred Blunt: 29, 66, 90, 159, 160; Lyndon Hayes: 26, 27, 74, 75; Eric Smith: 129, 133, 135, 137, 140, 149, 150, 151, 152, 153, 154, 157.

Photo acknowledgements
The Publisher would like to thank the following for their kind permission to reproduce their photographs:

(Key: b-bottom; c-centre; l-left; r-right; t-top)

123RF.com: 123vector 37 (car), 86br, agencyby 84/8, Diego Alies 37 (Book), andersonrise 148 (young girl with brown hair), AnnSunnyDay 37, Andrey Bayda 44tl, Jacek Chabraszewski 148 (young girl), Brian Eichhorn 148r (grandma), Elena Elisseeva 148 (son), Warren Goldswain 148 (mature man), Gabriel Gonzalez 121, goodluz 148 (father), Paul Michael Hughes 148 (young boy), Ihor Obraztsov 46r, jehsomwang 37 (wind), kritchanut 116-117 (background), Kurhan 148 (aunty), 148 (uncle), lammeyer 148 (mother), Lightwave Stock Media 32l, lightwise 117t, Roman Malyshev 37 (microscope), nazlisart 37 (Flag), Sean Nel 84/9, nyul 148 (brother), 148 (cousin), 148 (husband), Photoroad 8-9 (background), Aigars Reinholds 148 (grandpa), rido 148 (man), robinsphoto 148 (young woman), serezniy 84/1, Dmitriy Shironosov 148 (daughter), Andrei Shumskiy 7b (icon), 19b (icon), 31b (icon), 43b (icon), 55 (icon), 67b (icon), 79b (icon), 91b (icon), 103b (icon), 115b (icon), sima 148 (grandma), Eric Simard 148 (ME), sjenner13 96, David Smith 43r, 52-53 (balloon), Eunika Sopotnicka 33, stylephotographs 148 (mother-in-law), tetyanka 45 (car), veralub 84/3 (a), Mikhail Vorobiev 12b, Wavebreak Media Ltd 7l, 8c, Cameron Whitman 148 (sister), 148 (young man) , Lisa Young 148r (grandpa); **Alamy Images:** Vincent Abbey 87b, ableimages 48t, Agencja Fotograficzna Caro 94br, Arterra Picture Library 157/1, Anatolii Babii 62/C, Peter Barritt 103r, Creation of Adam fresco on the ceiling of the Sistine Chapel by Buonarroti Michelangelo Vatican Museum Rome Italy Europe 112-113b, Blend Images 59 (F), Catchlight Visual Services 91cr, 98tr, Cultura Creative (RF) 48b, Cultura RM 60, culture-images GmbH 65b, David J. Green - lifestyle 2 91cl, Deborah Ernest 61, Everett Collection Historical 103l, Garry Gay 43l, Ian Goodrick 55cr, 62/B, Tim Graham 110bl, Thierry Grun 87c, Heritage Image Partnership Ltd 104c, Images-USA 117 (bus), Isowork Images 62/E, Eddie Linssen 151t, LondonPhotos / Homer Sykes 108tr, M. Timothy O'Keefe 62/D, David Pearson 110tr, Davide Piras 43cl, 47/C, Pixellover RM 8 97, StreetStock 67cl, 71, The Illustrated London News Picture Library. Ingram Publishing. Alamy 110br, Gregg Vignal 10; **BBC Photo Library:** Hladik, Martin 36; **BBC Worldwide Ltd:** 16 (inset), 28 (inset), 40 (inset), 52l (inset), 55r, 64 (inset), 76 (inset), 100 (inset), 124r (inset); **Comstock Images:** 99; **Corbis:** 68 / Ocean 25 (background), 25cl, Amelie-Benoist / Bsip 31t, Andersen Ross / Cultura 52-53, Bettmann 23b, 81tr, 103cr, Edgar Su / Reuters 35l, Hemant Mehta / India Picture 87t, Jon Hrusa / Epa 24, Ingo Bartussek / Westend61 50r, Lan 80t, LWA / Larry Williams 16-17, Photo Media 67l, Photo Media / Classicstock 108l, Arnie Sachs / CNP / AdMedia 104l; **Fotolia.com:** 118, arphoto 44 (notes), Banana Republic 44-45 (background), Andrey Burmakin 79cr, Cifotart 80-81 (background), cunico 38tr; dominiquelavoie 151c, Dp3010 76 (cake), Esolla 77 (flowers), Eyematrix 56 (background), Fontanis 84/6, Joe Gough 84/11, Kaesler Media 38l, karandaev 84/10, Login 110 (background), Monkey Business 38r, nacroba 67cr, photorealistic 51, Željko Radojko 44 (watch), Raven 38 (food icon), Robsonphoto 76-77 (heart background), Maksim Striganov 44 (ring), sumnersgraphicsinc 77 (cork), surasaki 76-77 (flower background), Taiga 67r; **Getty Images:** 68/C, 112-113t, Frank Barratt 103cl, BBC News & Current Affairs / Jeff Overs 116l, Al Bello / Staff 88-89 (background), Bilderlounge 31cr, 38tc, Fotog 59/C, FPG 67t, George Hoyningen-Huene / RDA / Contributor 21 (F), Jeff Giniewicz 31r, 40-41, Tim Graham 163, Judith Haeusler 56b, Hero Images 34b, 47/A, Stan Honda / Staff 79r, 88-89 (foreground), iStock / Getty Images Plus 35c, Vincenzo Lombardo 115cr, Massive 68/A, Buda Mendes 9lt, Tatiana Morozova 69/E, Zhang Peng 119r, Philip Game / Lonely Planet Images 91r, 100-101, Photo 12 110tl, Photonica World 115cl, 119l, Tom C. Robison 43t, Terry Fincher 107, Westend61 68/B; **Nicola Krebill:** 56t; **NASA:** NASA / JPL / ASU 95; **Pearson Education Ltd:** Sophie Bluy 63; **Photolibrary.com:** Sugar Gold Images. Denkou Images 68/D; **Plainpicture Ltd:** Julian Love / Cultura 43cr; **Press Association Images:** Fiona Hanson 65cr; **Reuters:** Chip East 161, Dylan Martinez 79t; **Rex Features:** 19cl, 21 (B), 21 (G), 23t, 52r (inset), 80cr, 80bl, 104r, Agencia EFE 110cl, Ron C Angle 80br; Stuart Clarke 110cr, Cultura 84/3 (b), Cultura / REX

32r, Design Pics Inc 7r, 16b, Everett Collection 21 (D), I Love Images 115l, ITV 111, KeystoneUSA-ZUMA 81tl, Franck Leguet 21 (A), Geraint Lewis 83b, Steve Meddle / ITV 72, Scott Myers 21 (C), Niviere / Villard 21 (E), PictureGroup 79l, Brian Rasic 108br, Ron Sachs / Pool via CNP 21 (H), Solent News 47/B, Universal History Archive / Universal Images Group 81bl, 81br, WestEnd61 98tl; **Robert Harding World Imagery:** Nick Bonetti 93, Fernanda Preto 94cl, P. Schickert 91l, 92; **Science Photo Library Ltd:** Amelie-Benoist / Bsip 35r, David A. Hardy 31cl; **Shutterstock.com:** 06photo 122, 48c (butterfly), auremar 86tr, bikeriderlondon 86tl, Franck Boston 84/12, Andrey Burmakin 103t, damato 84/7, Zeynep Demir 19t, EpicStockMedia 59/E, Greg Epperson 84/5, FloridaStock 115r, 124-125, Stanimir G.Stoev 44 (coins), Jaroslaw Grudzinski 76 (rings/rose), InesBazdar 19cr, Inga Ivanova 151b, Shaun Jeffers 64-65, Christopher Kolaczan 157/5, Olivier Le Queinec 105r, M. Shcherbyna 157/2, mhatzapa 84/4 (b), Monkey Business Images 73, Vladimir Mucibabic 69/F, nobeastsofierce 104-105, Ollyy 12t, Pakhnyushcha 49, pixeldreams.eu 79cl, 83 (background), Graham Prentice 59/D, RG-vc 55cl, Rido 84/4 (a), robcocquyt 62/A, Sailorr 59/A, Sozaijiten 59/B, Ssuaphotos 157/3, Dan Thornberg 117 (flag), Three one five 157/4, Tupungato 94bl, Kiselev Andrey Valerevich 84/2, Roman Vanur 115t, Wavebreakmedia 31l, Chamille White 55t, Zurijeta 50l; **SuperStock:** Blend Images 98tc, Cultura Limited 7t, Cultura Ltd 14b, Cusp / Cusp 19r, 28-29, F1 Online 14t, RubberBall 7cr, Science Photo Library 7cl, 11l, 11r; **The Kobal Collection:** Warner Bros. / James, David 19l; **TopFoto:** 2005 155, Ronald Grant Archive / ArenaPAL 23c; www.playpumps.co.za: 55l, 56c

All other images © Pearson Education

CONTENTS

DVD-ROM: **BBC** DVD CLIPS AND SCRIPTS   ◗) BBC INTERVIEWS AND SCRIPTS   ▶ CLASS AUDIO AND SCRIPTS

CONTENTS

LISTENING/DVD	SPEAKING	WRITING
	talk about important dates in your life	write an email of introduction
listen to a set of instructions and do a test	talk about the differences beween men and women	
listen to three interviews	role-play an interview	
The Blind Painter: watch a BBC documentary about a blind artist	speak about yourself for 60 seconds	write a personal description
listen to a radio programme about films	talk about life stories	
listen to news reports	talk about an important news event	write a news report
listen to a woman telling a story	tell a true story or a lie	
Hustle: watch a BBC drama about an art thief	tell a narrative	write a newspaper article
listen to people making plans	discuss your plans and arrangements	write a series of messages
	talk about predictions	
listen to a series of misunderstandings	explain misunderstandings	
YouTube: watch a BBC documentary about the rise of YouTube	discuss how to create a video channel	write a proposal
	discuss how important becoming a millionaire is for you	
listen to people describing dream jobs gone wrong	talk about past habits	write a covering letter
listen to people making decisions in a meeting	participate in a meeting	
Gavin and Stacey: watch a BBC comedy about a man's first day in a new job	describe a day in your life	write about your daily routine
	talk about inventions over the last 100 years	write an advantages/disadvantages essay
listen to people answering difficult questions	present and answer questions on your area of expertise	
listen to conversations about technical problems	explain/solve problems	
Top Gear: watch a BBC programme about a race between a car and two people	present a new machine	write an advertisement

COMMUNICATION BANK page 83   AUDIO SCRIPTS page 87

)) LEAD IN

GRAMMAR

1 Read the text and find examples of ...

1 the past simple *he saw*
2 the past continuous
3 the present perfect
4 the past perfect
5 a modal verb
6 a superlative
7 a relative clause
8 a passive

There have been some amazing coincidences throughout history, but this might be the best. In 1900 King Umberto of Italy was dining in a restaurant when he saw that the owner looked exactly like him. The man, who was also called Umberto, was born in Turin on the same day as the king and, like the king, married a woman called Margherita. Amazingly, their weddings had been on the same day. The king invited the restaurant owner to an athletics meeting the next day. As the king sat down, he was told that the other Umberto had died in a mysterious shooting accident. Just as the king heard this news, an anarchist shot him dead.

PRONUNCIATION

2 A Find pairs of words that have the same vowel sound.

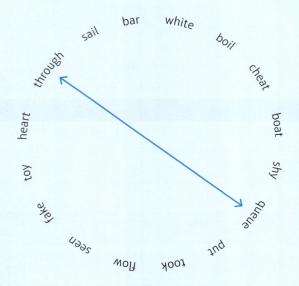

bar   white
sail   boil
through   cheat
heart   boat
toy   shy
fake   queue
seen   flow   took   put

B ▶ **L.1** Listen and check your answers.

C Work in pairs. Think of other words in English that use the same sounds.

VOCABULARY

3 A Complete the common phrases below using the correct verb from the box.

| ~~have~~ | take | check | watch | chat | go | meet |
| play | do (x2) | | | | | |

1 *have* a meeting   6 _____ some work
2 _____ your email   7 _____ on the internet
3 _____ out with friends   8 _____ a break
4 _____ some sport   9 _____ a DVD
5 _____ a colleague   10 _____ some music

B Add phrases 1–10 above to the word webs below.

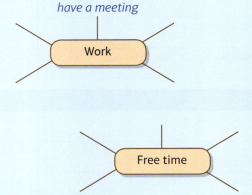

have a meeting

Work

Free time

C Can you add any more phrases to the word webs? Which of these things do you do on a normal day?

COMMON ERRORS

4 A Correct the mistakes.

1 She likes listening music.
2 I am architect.
3 Are you feeling allright?
4 When I can visit your house?
5 Let's discuss about this tomorrow.
6 He don't come here often.
7 We come from germany.
8 Where you go yesterday?
9 I live in this town all my life.
10 My wife is a really good cooker.

B Which mistakes are connected with ...

a) verb–noun agreement 6
b) spelling
c) verb tense
d) punctuation/capitalisation
e) prepositions
f) articles
g) vocabulary
h) word order
i) missing auxiliary verb
j) extra words

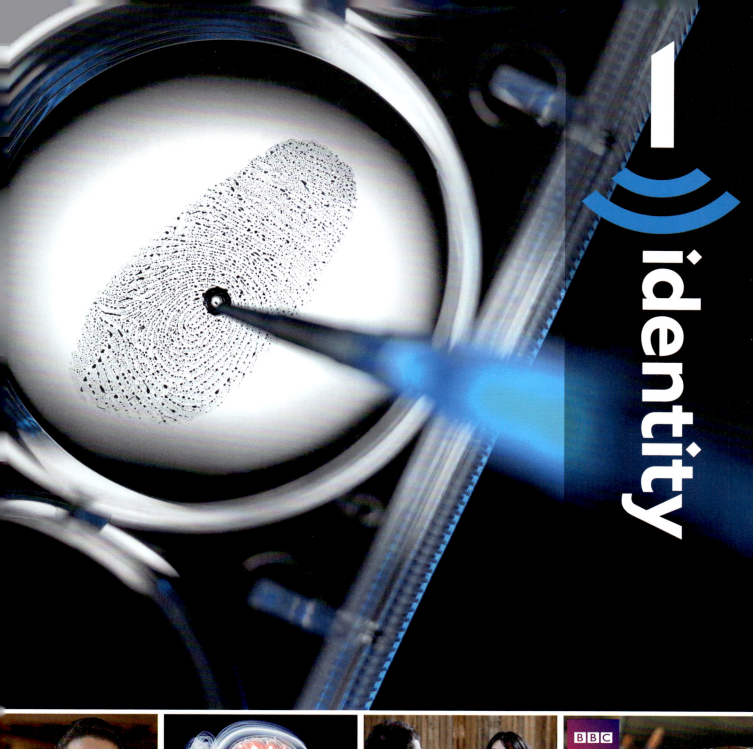

identity

E AND MY LANGUAGES p8

SAME OR DIFFERENT p11

TELL ME ABOUT YOURSELF p14

THE BLIND PAINTER p16

BBC INTERVIEWS

What does family mean to you?

1.1)) ME AND MY LANGUAGES

G question forms
P intonation: *Wh-* questions
V language

VOCABULARY

LANGUAGE

1 A Read questions 1–10. What do the words in bold mean? Check with other students or your teacher, then think about your answers to the questions.

1 Why are you learning English? For work, exams, travel, etc.?
2 Do you speak any languages apart from your **mother tongue** and English?
3 Who is the best language learner in your family?
4 Did you use any **learning strategies** when studying your second language? Which?
5 When was the first time you used a **foreign** language outside the classroom?
6 Do you have the chance to speak/write to **native speakers** regularly?
7 Is it important for you to learn **slang** or **jargon** in English, or do you only want to learn standard English?
8 Which is more important to you when you learn to speak a language: **fluency** or **accuracy**?
9 Which **skill** is the hardest for you: speaking, listening, reading, or writing? Which is the easiest?
10 Do you know anyone who is **bilingual**? What advantages might they have in life?

B Work in groups. Discuss your answers to questions 1–10.

2 Answer the questions.

1 Which words in bold in questions 1–10 have silent letters?
2 What are the silent letters in these words: *science, talk, listen, know, right, wrong, hours, guess*?
3 Which statement (a or b) do you think is true?
   a Most words in English are spelt differently to how they are pronounced.
   b Under twenty percent of words in English are spelt differently to how they are pronounced.

speakout TIP

Around fourteen percent of English words have irregular spelling; they are spelt differently to how they are pronounced. When you learn new words, try to hear them. Watch out for silent letters!

BILINGUALS: EXOTIC BIRDS OR EVERYDAY PEOPLE?

by Johan Acosta

Grandpa shouts, "Dinner's ready" in Danish. My mother asks me in English to lay the table. As I do so, I catch the theme tune of the Brazilian soap opera on TV in the living room, where my sister is relaxing. She speaks perfect Portuguese. My father asks her to record the programme in his native Spanish, and we take our places at the table. And what's on the menu? Italian meatballs.

We know we aren't a normal family. At any moment, you might hear conversations in four different languages, and almost everyone understands almost everything. But what is normal these days? My mother is half-Danish, half-English, and my father, who is from Bolivia, speaks Spanish and Guaraní. Because of my mother's work (she's now retired), we lived in Brazil, Italy and Germany, so we picked up three more languages. Now as adults, my sister and I both speak six languages.

READING

3 A Read the title of the text. What do you think it will discuss? Read to find out.

B Read the text again and answer the questions.

1 What six languages do you think the writer and his sister speak?
2 How do you think the writer learnt each of his languages?
3 How many of the world's people are thought to be bilingual?
4 What are those who learn their second language as children better at compared to those who learn a second language as adults?
5 What health benefit of being bilingual is mentioned in the text?

Being bilingual, or in our case multilingual, has so many advantages. All the recent research suggests we benefit in many ways: social, cultural, economic, academic, and intellectual. The research has also destroyed some of those persistent myths.

One of the myths is that bilingualism is uncommon, as if we bilinguals are like rare, exotic birds. The truth is that around fifty percent of the world's inhabitants are bilingual. The continents with the most linguistic diversity are Asia and Africa. In Nigeria alone, 500 languages are spoken, in India 400.

Some people believe that you have to learn both languages as a child to be truly bilingual. My sister and I are fortunate in this respect, but we know countless people who have mastered a second language as adults. They may not have such perfect pronunciation as those who acquire their second language as children, but they are still completely fluent and accurate.

Another myth about bilinguals concerns identity. Some people think we have split personalities. As kids, my sister and I were often asked "But where are you really from? Don't you get confused?" Not at all. I am me, the product of many cultures. I can switch languages easily, according to where I am and who I'm with, and this seems completely natural to me.

As for the benefits, bilinguals do better on certain tests, are better protected against mental illnesses such as Alzheimer's, gain insights into other cultures, have access to more of the world's information, and are in some contexts more employable. Being bilingual has made me who I am, and for that I'm grateful.

> One of the myths is that bilingualism is uncommon, as if we bilinguals are like rare, exotic birds.

C Underline words or phrases in the text that match meanings 1–6 below.

1 relating to the language you grew up speaking (paragraph 1)
2 learnt by listening/watching other people (paragraph 2)
3 speaking many languages (paragraph 3)
4 false ideas that people continue to believe and repeat (paragraph 3)
5 learn without needing to try hard, e.g. a language (paragraph 5)
6 understand important truths about a subject (paragraph 7)

D Discuss the questions with other students.

1 Do you agree with the writer's list of the advantages to being bilingual?
2 Do you think there any disadvantages to being bilingual?
3 Do you know any families that are bilingual or multilingual? Are they similar to the family in the text?

GRAMMAR
QUESTION FORMS

4 A Read sentences 1–6 and answer questions a)–e).

1 Do you <u>speak</u> other languages?
2 Did you use any learning strategies?
3 Who did you talk to?
4 What happened?
5 What did you talk about?
6 Who is the best language learner in your family?

a) Underline the main verb in each question. (The first has been done for you.)
b) Circle the auxiliary verbs. Which auxiliary refers to the past? Which refers to the present?
c) Which two questions are yes/no questions?
d) Which two questions end in a preposition: *of, by*, etc.?
e) Which two questions use *wh-* words to refer to the subject (the person who does the action, or the action itself) and don't use an auxiliary verb?

▷ page 68 **LANGUAGEBANK**

B ▶ **1.1** **INTONATION: *wh- questions*** Listen to the questions in Exercise 4A. Are the question words (*wh-* words) in 3–6 said in a higher or a lower voice?

C Listen and say the questions at the same time.

5 A Put the words in the correct order to make questions.

1 do / every / you / day / study ?
2 your / any / did / languages / teach / parents / you / other ?
3 is / learner / who / the / best / you / language / know ?
4 was / teacher / your / English / first / who ?
5 do / do / you / remember / what / English / to / words / in ?
6 languages / you / what / do / to / like / listening ?
7 do / what / watch / you / English / in / TV / programmes?
8 foreign / did / speak / first / when / language / a / you ?

B Choose three of the questions to ask other students.

SPEAKING

6 A Write four dates, four names and four places that are important to you.

Dates: *7 May 2008 – My son was born.*
Names:
Places:

B Work in groups. Take turns to explain what you wrote. As you listen, think of questions to ask afterwards.

WRITING

EMAILS OF INTRODUCTION; LEARN TO WRITE FORMAL AND INFORMAL EMAILS

7 A When would you write a letter or email to introduce yourself?

B Read the emails. Why are the people writing? Which sentences tell us?

To	ramirezh@languagestar.nett	Subject	Spanish conversation class

Hi Hernan,

My name's Julia Brown. I heard from my friend Nichola Lazarus that you're running a Spanish conversation class. She said you'd be happy to accept a few more people. My mother tongue is English but I picked up some Spanish years ago when I was travelling in Latin America. I really want to develop my fluency and accuracy, so I'd love to join the class. Hope to hear from you soon.

All the best,

Julia 😃

To	GND staff	Subject	Greetings

Dear Colleagues,

As you probably know, next month I will start work as the new director of the Language Teaching Education Programme. For those of you who don't know me, I would like to take this opportunity to introduce myself. Since 2010, I have worked at the School of Education at Borodive University. I have been involved in a number of language teacher education projects across Europe and I worked extensively on the Star Placement Initiative that placed six thousand native speakers in language classrooms in eight countries. I am married with two children and my family is bilingual in English and Turkish.

I look forward to working with you.

Yours sincerely,

Talya Osman

8 Read the five steps for good email writing. Do you think the emails in Exercise 7B follow steps 1–3?

1 **A**im for your **a**udience: think about who you are writing to. Is the email formal or informal?

2 **B**e **b**rief: try not to use too many words. Emails shouldn't go on for pages.

3 **C**ommunicate **c**learly: use simple, clear language and simple sentence structure.

4 **D**o two **d**rafts: write a first version and then rewrite.

5 **E**dit **e**verything: check grammar, vocabulary, spelling and punctuation before sending.

9 A Look at the emails in Exercise 7B again. Which one is formal and which is informal? How do you know?

B Answer questions 1–4 with formal (F) or informal (I).

1 Which email uses full forms of verbs (*I will, I would*) instead of contractions (*you're, I'd*)?

2 Which email leaves out words (e.g. *Hope to …* instead of *I hope to …*)?

3 Which email sounds more like spoken English?

4 Which email uses longer, more complex sentences?

C Complete the notes with phrases from the email.

> **Greeting**
> (formal):   ¹_____.
> (informal):   Hi/Hello.

> **Introduction**
> (formal):   I would like to take
>   this ²_____.
> (informal):   My name's …

> **Final message**
> (formal):   I look forward to …
> (informal):   ³_____.

> **Goodbye**
> (formal):   ⁴_____.
> (informal):   All the best.

10 Choose a situation below and write an email. Think about who you are writing to, the reason for writing and the style: formal or informal.

Situation 1
You are going to join an English conversation class. Write an email introducing yourself to the teacher and the class. Mention your experience of learning and speaking English and say why you want to join the class.

Situation 2
Next week you start a new job in a multinational company. Your colleagues speak over twenty languages, and all of them read English. Write to introduce yourself. Mention your previous work experience and the languages you know, and add something personal.

SAME OR DIFFERENT?

G review of verb tenses
P word stress
V relationships; collocations

((**1.2**

VOCABULARY

RELATIONSHIPS

1 A Work in pairs. Think of all the people you have talked to in the last 24 hours. What relationship do they have to you?

B Look at the words in the box and answer the questions.

> ~~boss and employee~~   classmates
> partner   team-mates   member
> godfather and godmother
> mentor and pupil   fiancée and fiancé

1 Which pair works together? *boss and employee*
2 Which pair promises to help guide a child through life?
3 Which pair is going to get married?
4 Which pair involves one person learning from the other?
5 Which word describes people who play in the same sports team?
6 Which word describes people who go to the same class?
7 Which word describes a person who is part of a club?
8 Which word is a general word for 'someone who you do something with'?

C ▶ 1.2 Listen to six sentences. Tick the words in the box in Exercise 1B which you hear.

D WORD STRESS Six of the words have two syllables. Find the words and underline the stressed syllable. Say the words aloud, putting the stress on the correct syllable.

▷ page 78 **VOCABULARY**BANK

speakout TIP

Remember: most two-syllable words in English have the stress on the first syllable. Hold a hand under your chin. Say the word slowly. The jaw (the bottom part of your chin) drops more on the stressed syllable.

2 Work in groups. Discuss the questions.
1 Can you think about one man and one woman who have played important roles in your life? Who were they? Why was the relationship important?
2 Do you think men and women are different in these roles? How?

LISTENING

3 A Read the text. Discuss. Do you think male and female brains are different? How? What are the stereotypes of men and women in your country?

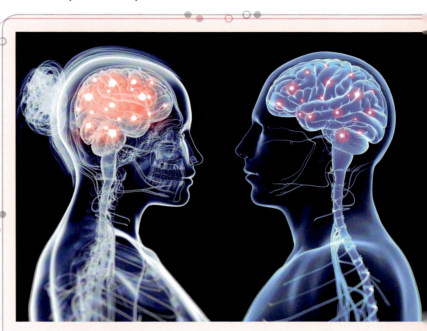

Are men's and women's brains
wired differently?

Is it true that men are from Venus and women are from Mars? Some researchers think that male and female brains are wired differently, with male brains wired from back to front, and female brains wired from side to side. This might explain why men are good at performing a single task, like cycling or navigating, whereas women might be better at multi-tasking. Other researchers disagree, however. What do YOU think? Try the bike test to find out if your brain is male or female.

B ▶ 1.3 Take a piece of paper. Listen to Part 1 and 2 and follow the bike test instructions.

C ▶ 1.4 Listen to the explanation in Part 3. Turn to page 83 and check your picture. How many parts did your bike have? Could it work? Does it have a person on it? Compare your picture with other students'.

D Discuss the questions.
1 Was the explanation correct for you?
2 Do you agree with the presenter's views about men and women?

❝ Women think people are important. Men, on the other hand, are more interested in getting the machine right. ❞

SPEAKING

4 A Read the information. Which comments do you agree/disagree with? Can you think of any opinions to add?

Are men & women really different?

We asked for comments and this is what you said.

"Absolutely! Men can't watch sport on TV **and** talk to their girlfriend at the same time."

"WOMEN DON'T KNOW HOW TO READ MAPS."

"Women remember **every outfit they've worn** for the past twenty years. Men **can't remember** what they were wearing yesterday without looking on the floor."

"Men can buy a pair of shoes on the internet in **90 seconds.** Women like to take three weeks."

"A baby is crying, a dog is barking, a doorbell is ringing, but the man of the house is sleeping. **Men can sleep through anything**. Women can't."

"Men speak in sentences. Women speak in **paragraphs.**"

B Do the men and women in your life conform to the normal stereotypes? Why?/Why not?

GRAMMAR

REVIEW OF VERB TENSES

5 A Match the underlined verbs below with the tenses a)–d).

1 We <u>asked</u> for comments and this is what you <u>said</u>.
2 Men can't remember what they <u>were wearing</u> yesterday.
3 Women <u>remember</u> every outfit they've worn for the past twenty years.
4 A baby <u>is crying</u>.

a) present simple
b) present continuous
c) past simple
d) past continuous

B Complete the rules with the correct tenses a)–d).

> **RULES**
> **1** We use _____ for actions, events or situations that are finished.
> **2** We use _____ for things that are going on at a particular moment in the present.
> **3** We use _____ for habits, routines and things that are always true.
> **4** We use _____ when someone was in the middle of an action at a particular moment in the past.

C Read about state verbs. Underline three examples in the text above.

> **RULES**
> Some verbs are not usually used in the continuous, e.g. want, like, remember, understand, know. These are called 'state verbs'.

▷ page 68 **LANGUAGEBANK**

6 A Read the text below and put the words in brackets into the correct tense.

> My name is Matsuko Tamazuri. I am twenty-three and I ¹_____ (be) a student. I study French and Spanish at university in Osaka, where I ²_____ (grow up), but at the moment I ³_____ (learn) English in New York. When I first ⁴_____ (get) here, everything ⁵_____ (seem) different: the food, the clothes and the weather. Now I ⁶_____ (enjoy) it and it feels like home! I have a boyfriend called Josh. I ⁷_____ (meet) him three weeks ago when I ⁸_____ (look) for an internet café! My hobbies ⁹_____ (be) surfing the net and singing. I ¹⁰_____ (sing) every day, usually in the bathroom!

B Work in pairs. Ask questions and write your partner's personal profile. Use the profile above to help.

VOCABULARY *PLUS*

COLLOCATIONS

7 A Work in pairs and do the quiz.

B Turn to page 83 and read the text to check your answers.

8 A Look at the quiz again. Find and circle five expressions using *take*, *get*, *do* and *go*.

B Write the expressions in italics in the correct places in the word webs below.

1 ~~on a diet~~, *home, off something, for a drink/a walk/ a meal, grey*

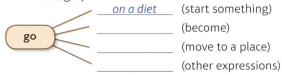

go	on a diet	(start something)
	_____	(become)
	_____	(move to a place)
	_____	(other expressions)

2 *responsibility for, after someone, part in something, a taxi*

take	_____	(go in a vehicle)
	_____	(join in)
	_____	(phrasal verbs)
	_____	(other expressions)

3 *married, a job/degree, on with someone, here*

get	_____	(become)
	_____	(obtain)
	_____	(go somewhere)
	_____	(phrasal verbs)

4 *exercise, research, housework, someone a favour*

do	_____	(activity)
	_____	(responsibilities and tasks)
	_____	(find information)
	_____	(help someone)

▷ page 78 **VOCABULARY**BANK

SPEAKING

9 A Think about your classmates. Write down the name of someone who:

- never gets angry.
- does research for his/her job.
- took a test in the last six months.
- went for a meal last weekend.
- took up a new hobby recently.
- always gets here early.
- went for a walk today.
- got a new job recently.

B Work in groups. Ask the other students to check if they agree with your ideas.

What women **really** think

Stella magazine commissioned YouGov, a research agency, to interview over 1,000 women in the UK about everything from their eating habits to their relationships and family values, to find out what they really think.

How do you think they responded?

How many women in the UK would prefer to have a male boss?
a) less than 30%   **b)** about 50%   **c)** over 70%

How many women spend more than seven hours a week doing exercise?
a) 4%   **b)** 15%   **c)** 30%

What is the biggest challenge for women today?
a) staying healthy   **b)** making enough money
c) balancing home and work life

What do women think is the best age to get married?
a) between 21 and 24   **b)** between 25 and 29
c) over 30

What do 59% of women think fathers should take more responsibility for?
a) their children   **b)** doing the housework
c) organising holidays

According to women, how much housework do they do?
a) more than 50%   **b)** over 75%   **c)** nearly all of it

How many women aged 45–54 met their husbands through the internet?
a) 1%   **b)** 9%   **c)** 16%

How many women have gone on a diet in the past?
a) 20%   **b)** between 35% and 45%   **c)** over 50%

F talking about yourself
P intonation: sounding polite
V interview advice

5 Tips to help you do well at interviews

How do you get into the university or the job of your dreams? Even before the interview, you might need to catch someone's attention. The Dean of Admissions at Harvard University says he often receives flowers and chocolates from potential students. One student sent references every day for three months. Eventually, he even sent a letter from his dentist saying how nice his teeth were. He didn't get an interview.

For those of you who do make the interview stage, here are five top tips:

1 Be prepared. Do some research about the university or company so you know what questions to ask.

2 Dress appropriately. You don't have to dress smartly but you should look clean. And don't wear 'bling' (large pieces of jewellery).

3 Arrive on time. Fifteen minutes early is OK.

4 Shake hands firmly and make eye contact. First impressions are important.

5 Speak clearly and try to offer full answers rather than short responses. This shows your enthusiasm.

SPEAKING

1 A Look at the photos. What types of interview could this be? Choose from the list below.

- job interview
- interview for a place at university
- newspaper/magazine interview
- interview for a talk show/radio programme
- placement interview for a language course

B Look at the list of interview types above. Answer questions 1–3.

1 Which types of interview above have you experienced?

2 Which will you experience in the future?

3 Do you think it is possible to show 'the real you' in a short interview? Why?/Why not?

VOCABULARY

INTERVIEW ADVICE

2 A Work in pairs. What should/shouldn't you do in an interview? Think of as many things as you can in two minutes.

You should try to ask questions.

B Look at topics 1–3 below and match them to the expressions in the box.

dress smartly *3*   speak clearly   answer briefly
shake hands firmly   send references
arrive on time   avoid eye contact   be prepared
do some research   show enthusiasm

1 Should do during an interview

2 Shouldn't do during an interview

3 Might do before an interview

3 Read the text and answer the questions.

1 What type of things do some people do to get an interview at Harvard University?

2 According to the text, what should you do before and during an interview? Do you agree with the advice?

FUNCTION
TALKING ABOUT YOURSELF

4 A ▶ 1.5 Listen to three extracts from interviews and answer the questions.

1 What types of interview are they?
2 Which interviewee doesn't follow the five tips? What does he/she do wrong?

B Answer questions 1–6. Listen again to check.

Interview 1
1 What does the student want to practise?
2 What types of classes are in the afternoons?

Interview 2
3 What did the girl organise on the summer camp?
4 What 'can be difficult' according to the interviewer?

Interview 3
5 What does the man want to know?
6 Why are online courses more difficult than face-to-face courses, according to the interviewer?

5 A Read the extracts from the interviews. Underline the expressions that introduce a question.

Extract 1
T: OK … Is there anything else?
S: Could I ask a question?

Extract 2
I: There are a couple of things I'd like to ask about. Your CV says you have some experience of looking after children?
A: Yes, I was a tutor on a summer camp last year.
I: Can I ask you about that? What type of things did you do?

Extract 3
I: I think that's about it. Do you have any questions? Any queries?
S: Um, yes, actually I do have a query.

B Read the extracts below and underline the expressions that are used to introduce an opinion.

Extract 1
S: I've … spent time in Britain, but that was a few years ago. So for me the most important thing is to just refresh …

Extract 2
I: OK. And you enjoyed it?
A: Yes.
I: What aspect, what part did you enjoy, would you say?
A: I suppose I'd have to say I liked the games best …
I: … We often find that different ages together can be difficult.
A: It depends. In my opinion, you can usually get the older children to help the younger ones.

Extract 3
S: So I wouldn't need to attend classes?
I: Not for the online courses. But … well, one thing I'd like to say is that the online courses are, in many ways, more difficult than face-to-face courses.

▷ page 68 **LANGUAGEBANK**

6 Put the words in the correct order to make sentences or questions.

1 query / I / a / have / do
2 I / a / could / question / ask / ?
3 like / couple / of / are / about / I'd / things / to / a / ask / there
4 ask / you / I / can / that / about / ?
5 true / this / opinion / my / isn't / in
6 to / I'd / I / agree / have / say
7 thing / that / like / I'd / one / say / is / to / is / course / the / difficult
8 is / thing / important / most / for / the / me / to / study

LEARN TO
USE TWO-WORD RESPONSES

7 A Match expressions 1–5 with expressions a)–e).

1 Of course.   a) Please continue.
2 That's right.   b) You're correct.
3 I see.   c) You're welcome.
4 No problem.   d) Yes, definitely.
5 Go ahead.   e) I understand.

B Which expressions in Exercise 7A are more formal? Read audio script 1.5 on page 87 to see how the expressions are used.

C ▶ 1.6 **INTONATION: sounding polite** Listen to the expressions in Exercise 7A. Notice how the speaker begins the expression with a high pitch to sound friendly. Listen again and repeat.

SPEAKING

8 Role-play an interview in pairs. Follow instructions 1–5.

1 Either choose one of the interview types in Exercise 1A, or Student A: turn to page 83 and Student B: turn to page 86.
2 Decide on your roles.
3 Interviewer: think of questions. You can make notes if you wish. Interviewee: guess what type of questions the interviewer will ask and prepare answers.
4 Practise your role-play.
5 Perform it in front of other students.

DVD PREVIEW

1 A Work in pairs and discuss the questions.

1 What creative or sporting activities are important to you? How would you feel if you couldn't do them any more?'

2 Which creative or sporting activities would be particularly difficult if you were blind? What problems do you think a blind person would have?

B Read about the programme. What caused Sargy Mann to go blind? What happened after he went totally blind?

The Blind Painter
BBC

Sargy Mann painted all of his professional life, first as a teacher and later as a professional artist. In his mid-30s he developed cataracts on both eyes, eventually leading to total blindness. He continued to paint. Twenty-five years later, Sargy's work was very popular with art collectors, with paintings regularly selling for more than £50,000 (US$80,000). He spoke to BBC News about his life and how he continued to work.

DVD VIEW

2 Watch the DVD. What does Sargy use to help him paint? What do you think of his paintings?

3 A Answer the questions.

1 What do you know about Sargy Mann after watching the clip?

2 Why did Sargy start to paint again after he went blind?

3 How does he use Blu-Tack to help him paint?

4 Who buys his artwork?

B Look at the quotes from the DVD. Try to complete the phrases using the words in the box.

> sensation go edgy coordinates landscape
> nonsense

1 The idea of painting when you were totally blind seemed a _____ to me.

2 I wonder what would happen if I give that a _____.

3 I had the most extraordinary _____.

4 Pre total blindness, I would say I was a _____ painter.

5 Now the thing about these bits of Blu-Tack of course is that what they are actually is _____.

6 They are _____, dangerous. They tell stories, they're full of impact through colour.

C Watch the DVD again to check your answers.

D Match the words and expressions from Exercise 3B with a)–f) below.

a) a very strange or unusual feeling

b) an artist who paints the countryside and scenery

c) experimental or avant-garde

d) numbers or information used to indicate a point

e) looked like a silly idea

f) (to) try something

4 Discuss the questions.

1 Do you think that Sargy Mann would have been such a successful artist if he was not blind?

2 Can you think of other people who have achieved great things despite physical disabilities?

speakout 60 seconds about you

5 A ▶ 1.7 Listen to Monica talking about herself. Which questions does she answer from the questionnaire below? What does she say?

Who are you?

1 What three words best describe you?
2 What is your idea of perfect happiness?
3 What possession is most important to you?
4 What is your greatest achievement?
5 What do you like most/least about your lifestyle?
6 What is your favourite sound, smell and taste?
7 What do you always carry with you?
8 Who would be your perfect dinner date? Why?
9 What's your favourite month and why?
10 If you could change one thing about the past, what would it be?

B Listen again. Complete the phrases Monica uses.

> **KEY PHRASES**
>
> I'm going to tell you _____ about myself.
> I think three words that describe me would be _____, talkative and hard-working.
> One of the things I _____ about my lifestyle …
> I suppose that's one _____ I don't like.
> In the summer, I love to _____ to the coast …
> It makes me feel _____.

C Prepare to talk about yourself for 60 seconds. Choose two or three questions from the questionnaire in Exercise 5A. Plan your answers. Practise and time your presentation to check you can say it all in just 60 seconds.

D Work in pairs and take turns to give your presentation. Take notes on your partner's presentation. What do you have in common?

writeback a personal description

6 A Read the text. What do you think are Stephan's main achievements?

Stephan Wilding in 100 words:

Stephan decided to change his degree from pharmacology to studying Thai at the School of Oriental Studies in London. When he finished university, he spent six months in Thailand teaching English before coming back to the UK. Unsure of his next move, he spent his evenings and weekends teaching himself how to code. He then got together with some friends to start up their own software business. It was a huge adventure and they learnt a lot very quickly. They have recently won a contract to build a computer platform for a design company, so the future is looking good.

B Work in pairs. You are going to write a short description of your partner. Check your notes from Exercise 5D and ask your partner questions if you think you need more information. Then use the text in Exercise 6A to help you write your description (100 words).

1.5)) LOOKBACK

V LANGUAGE

1 A Read the advice from a 1950's English course book. Complete the sentences with the words in the box.

> foreign   strategy   jargon   bilingual
> native speakers   ~~fluency~~   slang   accuracy
> skill   mother tongue

1 Using the right method, _fluency_ in the target language is possible after just a few weeks.
2 Students should talk with _____ _____ only. Exposure to other learners will result in new errors.
3 To improve _____, the student should copy out several pages from the textbook every day.
4 The student's biggest problem is translating every word of English into his _____ _____.
5 The best _____ is for the student to imitate the recordings for an hour at a time.
6 It is unnecessary to learn _____ words unless the learner needs them for a specific job.
7 It is impossible to become _____ unless the second language was learnt in childhood.
8 Students should avoid _____ because it isn't proper English.
9 To improve the listening _____, the student should listen daily to the radio.
10 The _____ student needs to be corrected every time he makes a mistake.

B Which advice is still useful? Change any advice you disagree with. Compare your ideas with a partner.

G QUESTION FORMS

2 A Find and correct the mistakes in the questions below. Four of the questions are correct.

1 When you started studying English?
2 Who did helped you to learn English?
3 What annoys you about your job or your studies?
4 Did you to learn anything important at school?
5 Do you be enjoy learning languages?
6 In your job or studies, is there anything you are not happy with?
7 When you imagine the perfect career, what do you think of?
8 What keeps you awake at night?

B Ask your partner four of the questions.

V RELATIONSHIPS

3 A Put the letters in the correct order to find the names of twelve types of people.

1 tomdogher   5 ceanife   9 sobs
2 niface   6 breemm   10 emeyloep
3 ilupp   7 stamcasel   11 trenom
4 nraterp   8 dethagorf   12 maatteme

B Work in pairs. Which of these people do you know or have in your life? Which of these are you?

G REVIEW OF VERB TENSES

4 A Find and correct the mistakes. Five of the underlined verbs are incorrect.

> **12.10.09**
>
> I ¹was walking to work this morning when I ²was seeing Mr Gonzalez, my old Spanish teacher. He ³was wearing a leather jacket and carrying a guitar. I ⁴ask him how he was. He said, 'Fine. I ⁵go to my band practice.' I said, 'What band?' He replied, 'I ⁶don't teach any more. It ⁷wasn't really the best job for me. A few years ago I ⁸was starting a band called The Big Easy. We ⁹don't make much money, but I ¹⁰'m liking the lifestyle.' I asked him where he lived and he said, 'I ¹¹'m living in my caravan at the moment. I ¹²travel a lot. I'm a child of the sixties!'

B Write a short diary entry about an interesting or unusual day.

F TALKING ABOUT YOURSELF

5 A Complete the conversations. Write an expression from the box in the correct place in the sentence.

> ~~query about~~   like to   to say   you about   I ask
> thing I'd

query about

1 **A:** I have a/the class. Do I have to bring a pen?
   B: No, it's a computer class.
2 **A:** Could a question? Where does the tennis class meet?
   B: At the tennis courts.
3 **A:** I'd have I'm not sure you're qualified. Why should we employ you for the library position?
   B: Because I'm good with children and animals.
4 **A:** There are a couple of things I'd ask. Firstly, can you work on Saturdays?
   B: Is that at the weekend?
5 **A:** One like to say is that you look good for your age. How old are you?
   B: Thirty.
6 **A:** Can I ask your latest film, *Philadelphia*? Where is it set?
   B: In Philadelphia.

B Work in pairs. Write an interview (a job, a place on a course, a magazine interview). Use the expressions in Exercises 5 and 7 on page 15 to help.

C Work in groups and take turns to role-play your interviews.

ONCE UPON A TIME...

2)) tales

FACT OR FICTION? p20

WHAT REALLY HAPPENED? p23

I DON'T BELIEVE IT! p26

HUSTLE p28

BBC INTERVIEWS

When is it ok to tell a lie?

2.1)) FACT OR FICTION?

G present perfect and past simple
P weak forms: *have*
V types of story; prepositions

SPEAKING

1 A Work in groups and discuss. Can you think of a film you have seen that has taught you about a person/event in history?

B Work in pairs and do the quiz. Decide if the information is fact, fiction or partly true. Then check your answers on page 83.

C Discuss. Do you think it is all right for film-makers to change the facts of a story? Why?/Why not?

HOLLYWOOD versus history

Can you tell your facts from fiction?

1 In the film *The Last Samurai*, Tom Cruise plays a US army captain who joins the samurai warriors in Japan in 1876. Was Captain Nathan Algren a real figure from history?

2 In *Shakespeare in Love*, William Shakespeare is inspired to write *Romeo and Juliet* by his real-life relationship with a young actress. Did this happen in real life?

3 In the film *Braveheart*, Mel Gibson plays the character William Wallace, leading an army of men with painted faces, and wearing kilts* as he battles to free Scotland from the English. How much truth is there in the story?

4 In the 1995 adventure, *Apollo 13*, we hear the pilot saying the famous words 'Houston, we have a problem.' But were these his exact words?

* kilt – a type of skirt traditionally worn by Scottish men

VOCABULARY
TYPES OF STORY

2 A Look at the types of film stories in the box below. Match the types of story with the descriptions a)–i).

a biopic   a docudrama   a disaster movie
a romantic comedy   a period drama
a fantasy film   a science fiction film
a psychological thriller   an action/adventure film
a mystery   a crime film

a) Heroes chase and fight each other.
b) The main character has mental problems.
c) A story about the science of the future.
d) Things that happen in the life of a real person.
e) The good guy (the detective) finds the bad guy (the criminal).
f) People dressed up in old-fashioned costumes.
g) Funny things happen. Two people fall in love.
h) Terrible things happen, but people survive.
i) A documentary made more interesting with some parts acted.
j) Strange things happen in an imaginary world.
k) Somebody gets murdered and a clever detective tries to find out who did it.

B Read the opinion below. What type of films does the writer enjoy? Why?

“ I love watching romantic comedies. I enjoy sitting down and watching a couple find each other and fall in love. It's really easy watching. I find it relaxing because I don't have to think. It's funny how my taste in films has changed. When I was younger I enjoyed action films, like *Terminator 2*. But now I guess my interests are different. ”

C Work in pairs and answer the questions.

1 Which types of film do you enjoy watching? Have your tastes changed over the years?

2 Can you name films which match each type of story? Have both of you seen them? Are your opinions about them the same or different?

LISTENING

3 A ▶ 2.1 Listen to the first part of a radio programme about films and answer the questions.

1 What type of film does the programme talk about?
2 Why are these films so popular?

B Work in pairs and discuss. Look at the photos of actors who have played the roles of famous people in films. How do you think they prepared for the roles?

C ▶ 2.2 Listen to the second part of the radio programme. Are the sentences true (T) or false (F)?

1 Helen Mirren won an Oscar for her role as the Queen.
2 Will Smith met Muhammad Ali but they didn't get on.
3 Josh Brolin talked to himself in a Texan accent all day.
4 Audrey Tautou watched films of Coco Chanel.

4 A ▶ 2.3 Listen to the whole programme and complete the information.

1 Hollywood has always used _____ _____ in its films.
2 Hollywood began making films in the _____s.
3 Some of the best films in recent years have been based on _____ _____.
4 From these films we've learnt about the _____ lives of some of the biggest music legends.
5 Many of these actors have won _____ for their roles.
6 Helen Mirren met the Queen for _____ .
7 Josh Brolin phoned hotels in Texas, to listen to their _____ .
8 Tautou wanted to look like Coco Chanel, so that we would recognise her _____ .

B Check your answers in the audio script on page 87.

A Helen Mirren B Queen Elizabeth I

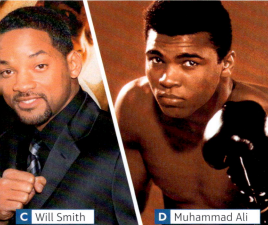

C Will Smith D Muhammad Ali

E Audrey Tautou F Coco Chanel

G Josh Brolin H George Bush

GRAMMAR

PRESENT PERFECT AND PAST SIMPLE

5 A Read the sentences in Exercise 4A and underline examples of the present perfect and past simple.

B Complete the rules with present perfect or past simple.

> **RULES**
>
> **1** Use the _____ to talk about experiences or things that happened before now. The time is not specified or important.
> **2** Use the _____ to talk about recent events, or an action which started in the past and continues now.
> **3** Use the _____ to talk about a specific event in the past (we know when the event happened).
> **4** Use the _____ to talk about an action which started and finished at a specific time in the past.

C Look at the sentences in Exercise 4A again and match them with one of the rules above.

▷ page 70 **LANGUAGEBANK**

6 A Read the text. What changed Chris Gardner's life?

> Chris Gardner is a successful businessman and a millionaire. But things ¹_____ always _____ (not be) easy. He ²_____ (not meet) his father until he was twenty-eight years old. This experience made him sure about one thing: he was determined to be a good father to his own children. As a young man, Gardner ³_____ (experience) hard times. His wife ⁴_____ (leave) him, he ⁵_____ (lose) his job, and at one stage he and his two-year-old son ⁶_____ (sleep) in train stations and airports. He ⁷_____ (come) a long way since then. His life changed when he ⁸_____ (meet) a man driving a red Ferrari and asked him what job he did. The man was a stockbroker, so Gardner asked him out to lunch, and the Ferrari driver introduced Gardner to the world of finance. Since he became successful, he ⁹_____ (spend) a lot of money helping homeless people, and he ¹⁰_____ also (write) books about his experiences. His story was told in the film *The Pursuit of Happyness*, starring Will Smith.

B Complete the text with the correct form of the verbs in brackets.

7 A ▷ 2.4 **WEAK FORMS:** *have* Listen to the pairs of phrases. Notice the difference.

1 I lived / I've lived **3** he decided / he's decided
2 we met / we've met **4** they spent / they've spent

B ▷ 2.5 Listen and write the sentences.

C Listen again and check. Then listen and repeat.

8 A Work in pairs. Student A: write *Have you ever … ?* questions using the prompts in the box below. Student B: turn to page 83.

> be on TV/in a newspaper watch film at an outdoor cinema
> do something embarrassing in public write a poem/story
> go to a country on a different continent
> collect something as a hobby see someone commit a crime

B Take turns to ask and answer questions. Try to find five things that you have done and your partner hasn't done.

SPEAKING

9 A Imagine you are going to make a film about your life. Choose five events you would like to include. Write some notes in the film strip below.

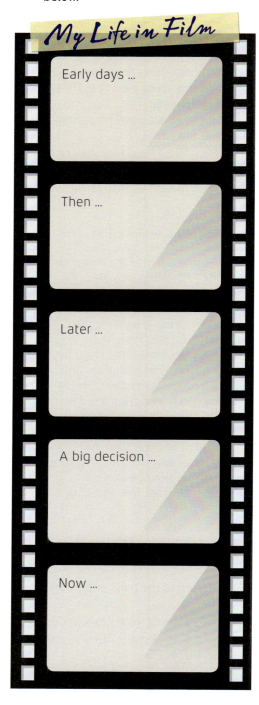

My Life in Film

Early days …

Then …

Later …

A big decision …

Now …

B Work in pairs. Take turns to talk about the film of your life.

C Think of three questions to ask your partner about the film of their life. Ask and answer the questions

Why did you choose to … ?
What happened when you … ?
What did you enjoy best about … ?

VOCABULARY *PLUS*

PREPOSITIONS

10 **PREPOSITION + EXPRESSIONS OF TIME** Complete the word webs with expressions in the box.

> Saturday   the weekend   Monday morning   New Year's Day
> July   the winter/the summer   the twenty-first century   lunchtime

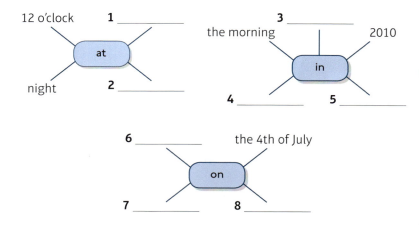

12 o'clock   1 _____

at

night   2 _____

3 _____
the morning   2010

in

4 _____   5 _____

6 _____   the 4th of July

on

7 _____   8 _____

speakout TIP

To help you remember which preposition of time to use, try to memorise this: **on** *Monday*; **in** *winter*; **at** *that* time.
on = for specific days, *in* = for time periods, *at* = for specific times

▷ Page 79 **VOCABULARY**BANK

11 **PREPOSITION + NOUN** Complete the phrases with the correct preposition: *on, for* or *by*.
1 It's a book _____ Dan Brown, a film _____ Steven Spielberg, a song _____ Amy Winehouse.
2 I saw it _____ TV. I heard it _____ the radio. I spoke to him _____ the phone.
3 We went _____ a walk, _____ a drive, _____ a run, _____ a swim.
4 They travelled _____ boat, _____ plane, _____ coach, _____ train.

12 A **FIXED EXPRESSIONS** Match the fixed expressions in bold in sentences 1–10 with meanings a)–j).
1 I dropped it **by mistake**.
2 I saw the film **on my own**.
3 He's here **on business**.
4 We met **by chance**.
5 It was made **by hand**.
6 We got there **in the end**.
7 She said it **on purpose**.
8 We arrived **on time**.
9 I'll do that **in a moment**.
10 They're **in a hurry**.

a) finally
b) cannot wait
c) by a person, not a machine
d) it was not a mistake
e) alone, not with other people
f) not early, not late
g) in a very short time
h) accidentally
i) not on holiday, but for work
j) it was not planned

B Look at Exercise 12A again. Write 6–8 questions with phrases with prepositions.

*Do you usually arrive **on time**, or are you sometimes late?*
*Do you prefer to live with someone, or live **on your own**?*

C Work in pairs. Take turns to ask and answer the questions.

WHAT REALLY HAPPENED?

G narrative tenses
P weak forms: *had, was, were*
V the news

2.2

SPEAKING

1 A Discuss the questions.

1 How do you keep up-to-date with the news?
2 What have been the most important stories in the last five years?

B ▶ 2.6 Listen to the excerpts from news reports. Which stories can you see in the photos?

READING

2 A Work in pairs. Read the definition and look at the photos below. Then answer the questions.

> **a conspiracy theory:** /kənˈspɪrəsi ˈθɪəri/ a theory or belief that there was a secret plan behind a major event

From Longman Active Study Dictionary.

1 What do you think the conspiracy theories were about (the events in the photos)?
2 Which story do you think involved a real conspiracy, according to official reports?

B Read the article to check your answers.

3 A Read the article again and answer the questions.

1 Who died in their bathroom?
2 Who was shot?
3 Who was arrested?
4 Who was murdered?
5 Who were the suspects?
6 Who was photographed?

B How are these words and phrases related to the stories?

> shadows   fans   stars   painkillers
> photographs   a studio   hospital
> the FBI (Federal Bureau of Investigation)
> a man with a gun   a flag

C Work in pairs. Answer the questions.

1 What do you think? Do you believe the official reports or the conspiracy theorists?
2 Do you know any other conspiracy theories? What happened?

The World's best-known conspiracy theories

Man on the Moon We've seen the photos, but many people claim that Neil Armstrong's 'giant leap for mankind' never really happened. They suspect that the astronauts Neil Armstrong and Buzz Aldrin never left earth, but acted out the scene and took photographs in a studio. Conspiracy theorists say there were strange shadows falling in the photos, and surprisingly no stars are visible. They point out that the US flag, planted by Buzz Aldrin, was apparently waving, although there is no wind on the Moon. However, these doubts can be explained logically. The lighting conditions on the Moon were complicated, and the flag only appears to 'flutter' because the astronauts moved it.

The King is Dead When Elvis Presley was found lying unconscious on his bathroom floor at his home *Graceland*, his family and friends desperately tried to save him. An ambulance was called and Elvis was rushed to hospital where a special room had been prepared for him. However, the 'King of Rock'n'Roll' was already dead when he arrived there. At first, doctors said that Elvis died because his heart had stopped, but later they claimed that drugs were involved. Elvis had taken painkillers because he had toothache and he couldn't sleep. However, for years his fans refused to believe that Elvis was gone, and there were numerous sightings of 'Elvis' around the world. There is even a website elvis-is-alive.com dedicated to finding out the truth.

The Death of a President President John F. Kennedy was assassinated on 22nd November 1963. He was riding through crowds in his car when a gunman shot him once in the head. Lee Harvey Oswald was arrested almost immediately after Kennedy's death, and charged with killing him. He was murdered two days later. A report in 1964 concluded that Oswald had acted alone. But conspiracy theorists have doubts, and believe more people were involved. Suspects include the CIA, the FBI and the Cuban leader Fidel Castro. In 1979, a new report agreed that Oswald had killed Kennedy, but also concluded that the President was killed 'as a result of conspiracy' by unknown people.

GRAMMAR
NARRATIVE TENSES

4 A Read the summary. Find and underline examples of the past simple and the past continuous and answer the questions.

> In 1963, President Kennedy and his team were preparing for the next presidential campaign. In Dallas, he was riding through crowds in his car when a gunman shot him.

1 Which tense is used to talk about the main events in a story?
2 Which tense is used to give background information in a story?

B Read the conclusion and answer the questions.

> Lee Harvey Oswald was arrested for the crime. A report later agreed that Oswald had killed Kennedy, but also concluded that there had been a conspiracy by a number of unknown people.

1 Which of the underlined verbs is in the past simple?
2 Which of the underlined verbs is in the past perfect?
3 Which tense describes the event(s) that happened first?

C Underline the correct alternative to complete the rule.

> **RULES**
> Use the past perfect to talk about actions which happened *before the past time event we are talking about/a very long time ago.*

D ▶ 2.7 **WEAK FORMS: had, was, were** Listen to the news summary. Notice how *was, were* and *had* are pronounced. Listen again. Try to shadow read the text (read at the same time as the recording).

were preparing /wə/ not /wɜː/
was riding /wəz/ not /wɒz/
had killed /həd/ not /hæd/

▷ page 70 **LANGUAGE**BANK

5 Read an account of an important news event. Complete the text with phrases a)–h).

a) He had been in prison
b) one of the branches broke
c) we heard some shots
d) 50,000 people were waiting
e) to hear what Mandela was saying
f) When he finally arrived
g) were talking to each other
h) many people had climbed onto it

11 February 2000: Nelson Mandela's release from prison
I was in the crowd on the parade in Cape Town that day. It was a hot day, and ¹_____ to see Mandela walk free from the prison. ²_____ for twenty-seven years. At one point ³_____ but most people stayed calm. People ⁴_____ and singing songs. There was a great feeling of solidarity. There was a large tree in the middle of the parade, and ⁵_____ to get a better view. Suddenly, ⁶_____ and people fell to the ground. But nobody wanted to leave. Nobody wanted to miss the chance of seeing Mandela for the first time. ⁷_____ there was a huge cheer. From where I was standing, it was difficult ⁸_____ but I knew I was there for an important moment in our history.

VOCABULARY
THE NEWS

6 A Match the headlines 1–8 with the explanations a)–h).

1 Actress survives **crash**
2 Politicians **attacked** by angry crowd
3 Student demonstration turns **violent**
4 Workers to **strike over pay**
5 Massive **earthquake** hits Italy
6 Most wanted **fugitive** arrested
7 Floods **destroy** crops
8 **Hostages** released after talks with rebels

a) Lots of angry people shout and throw things at some politicians.
b) People who were kept as prisoners are allowed to go free.
c) Police catch a man who they suspect committed a serious crime.
d) A natural disaster destroys part of a country.
e) A woman is involved in a car accident but doesn't die.
f) A lot of farmland is under water.
g) Many people might refuse to go to work.
h) People who are protesting begin to fight on the streets.

B Work in pairs. Describe some stories which have recently been in the news using the vocabulary in bold above.

speakout TIP

Headlines can be difficult. They contain incomplete sentences: articles and auxiliaries can be dropped, simple tenses are used instead of continuous or perfect tenses and the infinitive is used to talk about the future. Find examples in the headlines.

▷ page 79 **VOCABULARY**BANK

SPEAKING

7 A Choose one of the news stories in the lesson or another important news story. Make notes to answer the questions below.

1 What was the news story? Where were you when you heard the news?

2 What were you doing? Who were you with?

3 What did you think at first? How did you feel?

4 Did the news change things for you in any way?

B Work with other students. Tell them about your story.

WRITING

A NEWS REPORT; LEARN TO USE TIME LINKERS

8 A Read the news report and answer the questions. Underline the parts of the news report which help you to answer.

1 Who is the story about?   4 Where did it happen?

2 What happened?   5 When did it happen?

3 Why did it happen?   6 What is the situation now?

Fraud fugitive in Facebook trap

A man who was on the run from police in the US revealed where he was hiding through a series of Facebook updates. Cameroon-born Maxi Sopo falsely obtained credit from banks while he was living in the US. By the time he had finished, he had stolen more than $200,000. He then escaped to Cancun in Mexico, where he was happily spending the money, until he made posts on his Facebook page telling the world that he was 'living in paradise'.

'He was making posts about how beautiful life is and how he was having a good time with his buddies,' said Assistant US Attorney Michael Scoville. 'He was definitely not living the way we wanted him to be living, given the charges he was facing,' he added.

However, during his time in Cancun, Mr Sopo also befriended a former justice department official on the networking site. This man, who had only met Mr Sopo a few times, was able to discover exactly where Mr Sopo was living. As soon as he had this information, he passed it to the Mexican authorities who arrested Sopo last month.

The twenty-six-year-old is currently in custody in Mexico City.

B Read the news report again. Find examples of the following:

1 quotes used to give someone's opinion

2 a concluding statement which gives us information about the current situation

3 an introductory statement which explains in one sentence what happened

4 more information about the background to the story

9 A Look at the news report and find examples of the time linkers in the box.

> as soon as   while   during   until
> by the time

B Look at the words/phrases in the box above. Which time linker do we use to link an action that:

1 happened previously?   _by the time_

2 continues up to that point and then stops?

_____

3 happens at the same time as another action?

_____

4 happens at some point in a period of time?

_____

5 happens immediately after something else has happened?

_____

C Complete the sentences with the correct time linker.

1 I came _____ I heard the news.

2 They arrived _____ we were having dinner.

3 Her cat died _____ the night.

4 We waited _____ the lights had gone out.

5 _____ the fire engines arrived, the house was destroyed.

10 A Work in pairs. Choose a headline and write six questions asking for information about the story.

> Actress survives crash

> Politicians attacked by angry crowd

> Man shot outside his house

B Give your questions to another pair of students.

C Look at the questions and use them to write a short news report (100–150 words). Use the ideas in Exercise 8B to help you.

D Compare your stories with other students. Who has the best story?

2.3)) I DON'T BELIEVE IT!

F telling a story
P intonation: sounding interested
V say/tell

VOCABULARY

SAY/TELL

1 A Work in pairs and discuss. How do you know when someone is lying? Do you think their behaviour changes?

B Read the text to check your answers.

How do you know if someone is lying?

From little white lies to lies which can destroy nations, people have lied for as long as they have told the truth. Some people are very good at it. So, how do we know if someone is lying?

Here are the things to look out for

1 The guilty hand: when someone is telling the truth they usually use more body language. They move their hands and their face more. When someone lies, their hands are still.

2 The lying eye: people find it very hard to tell you a lie if they're looking at you straight in the eyes. Normally, they look away just at the moment that they tell the lie.

3 The 'Me': when people tell a story about themselves, they tend to use a lot of 'me' words, like I, me, and my. When they tell a lie, they don't use the 'me' words as much.

2 A Match 1–6 with a)–f) to make sentences.

1 I'm terrible at telling
2 My brother told me
3 I think you should say
4 Sometimes it's better to tell
5 You should just say
6 I said

a) 'hello', but she didn't answer.
b) a white lie than to upset someone.
c) what you mean.
d) a funny story yesterday.
e) sorry.
f) jokes. I always forget the punch line!

B Add the phrases with *say* and *tell* from Exercise 2A to the table.

Say	Tell
'hello'	*a story*

C Work with other students. Do you agree/disagree with the statements? Why?

1 A lie can travel half way around the world while the truth is putting on its shoes.
2 A good storyteller should mix fiction with truth to make their stories interesting.
3 It's OK to tell lies sometimes.

A

FUNCTION

TELLING A STORY

3 A Look at the pictures above which tell a story. They are not in the correct order. What do you think is happening in each picture?

B ▶ 2.8 Listen to a woman telling her story. Number the pictures in the correct order.

4 A Look at the phrases we can use to help tell the sequence in a story. Add the sequencers from the box to the correct place in the table.

This happened when   The next thing I knew
Anyway,   In the end,   Before long,
And then, all of a sudden

beginning
In the beginning, …
This happened when

describing what happened
Well, …
So, …

ending
So, …
Finally, …

B Listen to the story again, and tick the phrases you hear. Check your answers in the audio script on page 88.

▷ page 70 **LANGUAGE**BANK

5 A Work in pairs. Practise telling the story using the sequencers and the pictures to help you. Start like this:

This happened when the woman had an important interview and …

B ▶ 2.9 Do you think the woman was telling a true or false story? Listen to find out.

LEARN TO

SHOW INTEREST

6 A Look at phrases a)–j). Which phrases complete extracts 1–6?

a) what happened then?

b) What did you do?

c) Then what?

d) Oh no!

e) Oh dear.

f) How embarrassing!

g) That's really funny.

h) Really?

i) You're joking!

j) You're kidding!

1 W: So, anyway, erm … I then got on to the tube, um … to go for my interview.

   M: Right, and ___*a*___

2 W: I've woken up shouting the word, 'Mum!'.

   M: No! _____

3 W: At the top of my voice, in a packed, quiet tube.

   M: _____

4 W: … they're looking at me in a rather strange way.

   M: Right … _____

5 W: My face had swollen up! … And it was bright red, … and covered in blotches, spots …

   M: Oh! _____

6 W: Yes, and the pills that my mother had given me were so out-of-date that they had caused an allergic reaction …

   M: Oh! … _____

B ▶ **2.10** **INTONATION: sounding interested** Listen and check your answers. Notice how intonation is used to sound interested. Is it high or low?

C Listen again and repeat the phrases. Try to sound interested. Then repeat but try to sound bored. Can you hear the difference?

speakout TIP

When someone tells a story, try to use comments and questions to show that you are interested e.g. *How amazing!* Remember to check your intonation. Do you sound interested?

SPEAKING

7 A Prepare to tell a story. It can be a true story or a lie. Choose one of the situations below. Talk about when you:

- got stuck in a lift
- missed (or nearly missed) a flight
- lost something valuable
- spoke to someone famous
- got a tattoo
- went swimming at night
- were mistaken for someone else
- slept outside
- tried a very dangerous sport
- found something unusual

B Think about the details of your story. Think about the questions below and make some notes or practise telling your story. Try to use some of the sequencers from Exercise 4.

- Where were you?
- Why were you there?
- What were you doing?
- What happened?
- How did you feel?

C Work with other students. Take turns to tell your stories and listen and respond. Ask questions to decide if it is a true story or a lie.

A: I once got stuck in a lift.
B: Really?
A: Yes. I was …

D Tell the other students if it is a true story or a lie.

DVD PREVIEW

1 Work in pairs. Discuss the questions.

1 Which famous fictional thieves/ investigators/detectives do you know about?
2 Which are famous in your country?
3 Do you watch any crime detective dramas? Which ones? What do you like/dislike about them?
4 What are the features of good detective dramas, e.g. interesting characters?

2 Look at the pictures and read about the programme. What problems do you think Finch had when he stole the painting?

Hustle

BBC

Hustle is a BBC drama series about a team of criminals who try to obtain and sell things in an illegal or dishonest way. In this programme we meet Finch, a burglar. He's in trouble with Customs, who believe that he has stolen a valuable piece of art. Unfortunately for Finch, when he stole the painting, things didn't go quite according to plan.

DVD VIEW

3 A Watch the programme. What problems did Finch encounter?

B Match the words in the two columns to make common crime collocations. Work with your partner. What do these words mean?

1 guard   a) thief
2 art   b) guard
3 valuable   c) weapon
4 burglar   d) officer
5 customs   e) dog
6 loaded   f) alarm
7 security   g) painting

C Tick the things above which you see in the clip. Which of the above do you not see?

4 A Work in pairs and answer the questions.

1 How does Finch get into the grounds of the mansion?
2 What is the security guard doing?
3 What does Finch do when he breaks into the house?
4 Why does Finch have to run with the artwork?
5 How does Finch escape?
6 What happens at the airport?
7 Why do customs officers search Finch? Do they find anything?
8 What do customs plan to do?

B Watch the DVD again to check.

C Discuss what you think Finch does next. What do you think will happen?

speakout a narrative

5 A Work in groups. Look at the pictures. What do you think happened?

B ▶ **2.11** Listen to someone telling the story. Do you think the story is true?

C Listen again and tick the key phrases you hear.

> **KEYPHRASES**
>
> This story is about …
> The problem was that …
> In fact, …
> What he didn't realise/know was that …
> However, …
> Later, …
> Because of this, …
> In the end, …

6 A Work in pairs. Take turns to retell the story using the key phrases.

B Work in pairs. Student A: look at the picture story on page 84. Student B: look at the picture story on page 85. Use the phrases in Exercise 5C to tell your partner what happens in your story.

writeback a newspaper article

7 A Read about a famous art theft. Who stole the painting? Why did he steal it? What happened in the end?

Famous painting stolen

On 21st August, 1911, Leonardo da Vinci's Mona Lisa, one of the most famous paintings in the world, was stolen from the wall of the Louvre Museum, in Paris. At first, the police thought one of the guards might have stolen the painting, but seventeen days after the theft, they arrested poet Guillaume Apollinaire. However, he was released when police could find no evidence that he had committed the crime. Two years later, the real thief, Vincenzo Peruggia, was arrested in Italy. Peruggia had worked at the museum, and had stolen the painting because he was angry about how many Italian paintings were on display in France. He had planned to return the painting to the Italian Uffizi gallery, in Florence. The public was so excited at the news of finding the Mona Lisa that the painting was displayed throughout Italy before it was returned to France in 1913.

B Write up the story of Finch's art theft as a newspaper article, using the article above and the key phrases to help you.

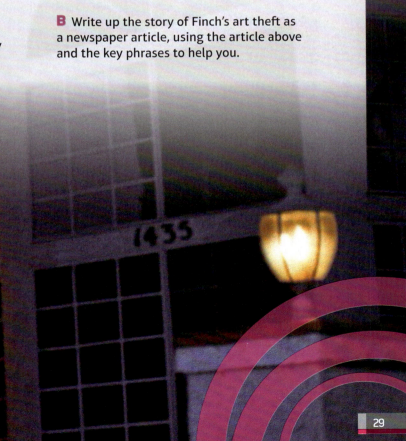

(V) TYPES OF STORY

1 A Add the missing letters to complete the types of story.

1 One of my favourite a_ _ _ _ _ films of all time is *The Terminator*.
2 Jamie Foxx stars in *Ray*, a great b_ _ _ _ _ of Ray Charles.
3 *Pretty Woman*, starring Julia Roberts and Richard Gere, is my favourite r_ _ _ _ _ _ _ c_ _ _ _ _.
4 I'm not a great fan of p_ _ _ _ _ d_ _ _ _ _, but I thought this production of *Jane Eyre* was brilliant.
5 I loved the p_ _ _ _ _ _ _ _ _ _- t_ _ _ _ _ _, *Silence of the Lambs*, but I found it very scary.
6 I still enjoy Agatha Christie's *Murder on the Orient Express*. It's one of the best ever d_ _ _ _ _ _ _ films.
7 I can't watch s_ _ _ _ _ _ f_ _ _ _ _ films, like *Star Wars* and *Alien*. I can't stand them.
8 I think d_ _ _ _ _ _ _ _ _, films like *Nixon*, are a great way to learn about what really happened during important events.

B Choose your three favourite film genres. Find other students who like the same genres and work together to make 'best ever' lists of the films in those genres.

(G) PRESENT PERFECT AND PAST SIMPLE

2 A Look at the phrases below. Have you done any of these things? Write sentences using *I've …* , *I haven't …* and *I have never … .*

- see a famous band
- ride a horse
- visit another country
- run a marathon
- start a business
- travel on your own
- write a diary/blog
- organise a big family party
- play in a band/write a song
- walk in the mountains/go skiing
- swim with dolphins/go scuba diving
- meet someone famous
- go to university/change your job

B Choose one thing you have/haven't done and tell your partner more about it.

I've played in a band. When I was at university I played in a band called 'The Hooligans'.

(G) NARRATIVE TENSES

3 A Put the verbs in the correct tense to complete the story.

Sasha [1]_____ (wake) up late because she [2]_____ (forget) to set her alarm clock. She [3]_____ (have) breakfast when the telephone [4]_____ (ring). It was her boss. He wanted to know why she [5]_____ (not finish) the report that he [6]_____ (ask) her to do. She quickly [7]_____ (leave) the house to go to work. She [8]_____ (stand) on the train when she noticed that lots of people [9]_____ (look) at her feet. Then, she [10]_____ (realise) that she [11]_____ (forget) to put her shoes on. She [12]_____ (wear) her slippers.

B Can you remember a day when you woke up late? Why? What happened? Tell your partner.

(V) THE NEWS

4 A Underline the correct option to complete the headlines.

1 Postal *destroy/strike* causes huge delays
2 Police attacked during student *demonstration/crash*
3 *Fugitives/Hostages* released after negotiation with rebel leader
4 Hundreds homeless after *earthquake/violent* hits
5 *Fugitive/Flood* found hiding in forest
6 Train *strike/crash* kills sixty people
7 House *attacked/crashed* with petrol bomb

B Work in pairs. Choose two or three of the headlines in Exercise 3A. Write mini news stories giving more details about each story.

(F) TELLING A STORY

5 A Add a word to each speaker's part to correct the conversations.

    happened
1 A: This/when I was living in Hong Kong.
  B: Oh really? happened?
2 A: I was having a shower when all a sudden I saw a huge spider.
  B: Oh no. What you do?
3 A: Anyway, before I knew it someone called the police.
  B: Really? What next?
4 A: The next I knew, the man was running towards me and shouting.
  B: don't believe it!
5 A: , anyway I was going up the ski-lift and I fell off.
  B: embarrassing!
6 A: So, in end, I had to pay all the money back.
  B: dear.

B Work in pairs. Choose three of the conversations above and expand the stories.

C Work in groups. Take turns to role-play your conversations.

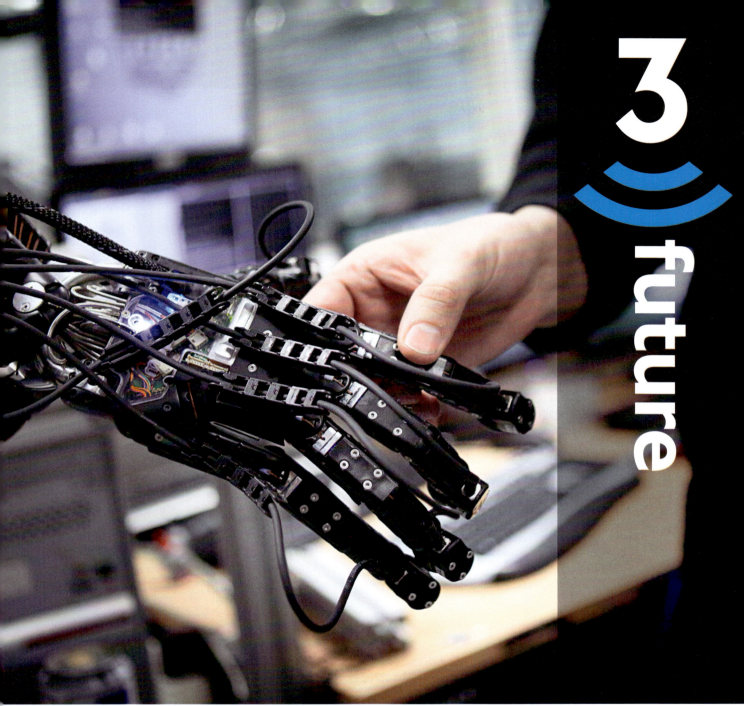

3)) future

MAKING PLANS p32   **TOMORROW'S WORLD** p35   **IN OTHER WORDS …** p38   **YOUTUBE** p40

SPEAKING **3.1** Discuss your plans and arrangements **3.2** Talk about predictions
      3.3 Explain misunderstandings **3.4** Discuss how to create a video channel

LISTENING **3.1** Listen to people discussing making plans **3.3** Listen to a series of
      misunderstandings **3.4** Watch a BBC documentary about the rise of YouTube

READING **3.2** Read an article about the future

WRITING **3.1** Write a series of messages **3.4** Write a proposal

BBC INTERVIEWS

Can new technology help communication?

G the future (plans)
P fast speech: *going to*
V organisation

VOCABULARY
ORGANISATION

1 A Work in pairs. Read the introduction to the questionnaire. Are you a planner or a procrastinator?

B In pairs ask and answer questions 1–4 in the questionnaire. Do you have similar answers?

C Find phrases in bold to match the definitions below.

1 not pay attention to the things you are supposed to be doing
2 delay (a job)
3 spend time doing things that aren't important
4 put jobs in order of which is most important
5 do lots of different jobs at the same time
6 complete tasks
7 do jobs just before the time they need to be done
8 do things in advance
9 be careful with your time
10 begin a job

D Work in groups. Answer the questions.

1 When was the last time you left something until the last minute?
2 Can you think of a job that you have put off for a while? When do you plan to do it?
3 What do you get distracted by when you're working? How do you try to avoid distractions?
4 Do you think it's a good idea to write to-do lists?

▷ page 80 **VOCABULARYBANK**

LISTENING

2 ▶ 3.1 Listen to three people discussing the questionnaire. Which of the following topics do they not talk about?

> making plans   holidays   writing lists   work arrangements for tonight

3 A Work in pairs. Can you complete these sentences from the listening?

1 You generally like to do things ahead of _____.
2 It's the only way to get _____ done.
3 You might need to change your _____, so why bother making plans in the first place?
4 I much prefer to _____ and see what happens.
5 This evening a _____ of mine's coming over.
6 I'm going to try out a new _____ recipe.
7 I'll see how I _____. I might go out, or I might just stay at home and _____.
8 I do get jobs done, but I never get started _____ away.

B Listen again to check your answers.

C Discuss. Who would you prefer to work with, Laurie, Kenna or Javier? Why?

Are you a planner or a procrastinator?

Do you plan your day or do you prefer to see what happens? A planner will spend the night before work making lists, prioritising, and making sure everything is under control. They arrive early and get started on their first task. A procrastinator, on the other hand, is more likely to arrive at work just in time, with a coffee and breakfast in their hand and a stressed look on their face.

When you have a job to do, or you need to **meet a deadline**, do you:

1 generally **do things ahead of time** or **leave things until the last minute**?

2 prefer to **get started** on a difficult job or **put off** doing difficult jobs until later?

3 tend to **get distracted** easily and **waste time** or do you **use your time wisely** and **get things done**?

4 write to-do lists and **prioritise tasks** or do you prefer to **multitask**?

GRAMMAR

THE FUTURE (PLANS)

4 Read the conversation and find examples of the structures described below.

Kenna: This evening a friend of mine's coming over. We're eating at my house – I'm going to try out a new pasta recipe. And then we're going to the cinema to see that new Argentinian film.

Laurie: Javier?

Javier: Uhhh … I don't really know. I'll see how I feel. I might go out, or I might just stay at home and relax. I told you, I really don't like to plan.

> **RULES**
>
> **1** Use present continuous to talk about plans or arrangements which have already been made, e.g. *A friend of mine is coming over.*
> **2** Use *going to* + infinitive without *to* to talk about a plan or intention. You have decided that you want to do this, but you may not have made the arrangements, e.g. _____
> **3** Use *might* + infinitive without *to* when you are undecided or not sure what the plan is, e.g. _____
> **4** Use *will* + infinitive without *to*, to talk about the future when you have no specific plan, or you make the decision at the time of speaking, e.g. _____

▷ page 72 **LANGUAGE**BANK

5 A ▶ 3.2 Listen and complete the sentences.

1 What _____ at the weekend?
2 We _____ my brother and his family.
3 Where _____ for them?
4 They _____ a party on Friday.
5 _____ with us tomorrow?
6 I'll ask Marion when she _____ .

B FAST SPEECH: *going to* Listen again. Notice how the speakers sometimes pronounce *going to* /ɡənə/ in fast speech. Tick the sentences where *going to* is pronounced /ɡənə/.

C Listen again and practise saying the sentences fast.

What are you going to do at the weekend?

6 Underline the correct alternatives to complete the conversation.

Pete: Hey Dax. What [1]*are you two doing/will you two do* on Saturday night?

Dax: I don't know. We [2]*might/will* go to the Death City Dread concert. What about you?

Pete: [3]*I'll have/I'm going to have* a bit of a party. My parents [4]*are going/will go* away for the weekend, so I've asked a few people to come over to my place. Kris [5]*will bring/is bringing* his DJ equipment round, so [6]*we're having/we'll have* music. And everyone [7]*is going to bring/might bring* some food and drink. Euan [8]*will come/is coming* with a few friends. Do you think you can make it?

Dax: It sounds great. [9]*I'm going to text/I'll text* Leyla to ask her what she thinks. Then [10]*I'm calling/I'll call* you back to let you know. Is that OK?

Pete: That's fine. [11]*I'll speak/I'm going to speak* to you later. Bye.

7 A Write sentences for situations 1–6 below. Think about whether you have made arrangements already, then decide which tenses to use.

1 something you plan to do at the weekend
Some friends are coming to stay. (I've already arranged this.)
I might go out for a pizza on Friday night. (I don't know yet.)

2 something you are going to do after the class
3 something you might buy in the near future
4 something that someone in your family is planning to do
5 a plan or ambition you have, related to your work/studies
6 something that you plan to do for your next holiday

B Work in pairs. Compare your ideas. Ask and answer questions to find out more information.

A: My sister's moving to Poland.
B: Really? That sounds exciting. Which city?

SPEAKING

8 A Think about two or three plans or arrangements with other people that you have made recently. Use the questions below to make some notes.

1 What is the plan?
2 Who is involved?
3 How did you communicate to make the arrangements?

B Work in groups. Tell the other students about your plans and how you made the arrangements. Do you have similar or different ways of organising yourselves?

WRITING

MESSAGES; LEARN TO USE NOTE FORM

9 Work in pairs. Look at messages 1–4 and answer the questions.

1 What do you think the relationship is between the writer and the person they're writing to?
2 Are the messages formal or informal?

Leyla
Gone to the dentist.
Be back at 4p.m.
Jen

Pete
Please call Tricia on
07679 437 562 asap
Lucy

Hope you enjoyed
the concert.
Dinner's in the oven.
F X

Can you pick us up
from football tonight?
See you later
Ben + Max

speakout TIP

Leave it out! When we write notes and messages we don't always write complete sentences. We often miss out small grammatical words to make the message shorter.

10 A Look at messages 1–4 in Exercise 9. The words in the box have been left out. Which message do they belong to?

> I   We'll   Your   I've   Can you   I'll

B Rewrite messages 1–4 below using fewer words.

1
> Are you feeling hungry? Do you want to meet me for lunch at Pavarotti's 1p.m.? Rx

2
> We're going to see Elton John in concert. Would you like me to book you a ticket? Tonya

3
> Pete called to say that he won't be able to come to dinner. Do you think you could call him back on 01954 627 823? Thanks. Jayne

4
> I'm really sorry but I can't come to the cinema tonight because I've got too much work to do. I hope you enjoy the film. Bess

11 Write short messages for the situations below.

1 You're going away for the weekend and would like your flatmate to water the plants.
2 You want to invite a classmate to the cinema.
3 You need to apologise to a work colleague for missing a meeting.

TOMORROW'S WORLD

G the future (predictions)
P stress in time markers
V future time markers; idioms

3.2

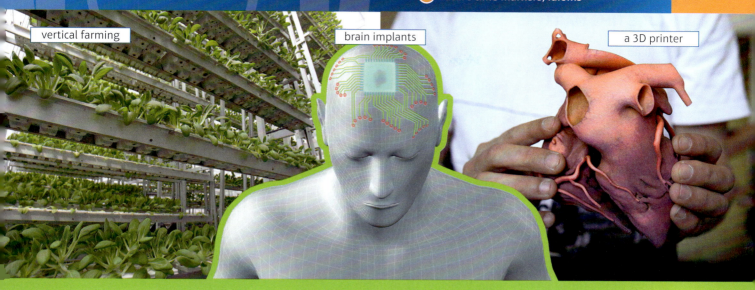

vertical farming

brain implants

a 3D printer

READING

1 Look at the photos and answer the questions.

1 What inventions or developments do the pictures show?

2 How do you think they can benefit people?

2 A Read the article. What does it tell us about the things shown in Exercise 1? What predictions does it make about translating machines and nano monitors?

B Complete the summary of the article with words from the text. Use one word in each gap.

The writer believes a machine will be able to ¹_____ our words into different languages. She thinks we'll use monitors in our ²_____ to check our health, and 3D printers will make perfect ³_____ of human organs like the heart. We will entertain ourselves with virtual reality, as computers learn to interact with the ⁴_____. The problems caused by ⁵_____ change will mean vertical farming becomes popular.

C Discuss with other students.

1 Which ideas in the article do you like? Can you think of other uses for these inventions?

2 Which ideas don't you like? Why not?

3 Which ideas do you agree will probably come true?

A better world?

Communication

In the near future, we may be able to communicate in any language we choose. A number of companies are working on translating machines that use the voice frequencies of the speaker. This makes it sound as though the user is speaking the foreign language. We already have translating machines, but they are slow and inaccurate and they sound like robots. In only a year or two this new machine, which will be a headset, could come onto the market and allow us to speak every language under the sun.

Health

The future of health is going to be a tale of big and small. Tiny nano monitors will be placed inside our bodies, and these will produce Big Data – enormous amounts of information – that allow us to check our health and help us predict illnesses. Another big development probably won't be ready in the short term, but in the long term there is hope that 3D printers will make copies of body parts such as hearts, livers and kidneys. If it happens, this is likely to save millions of lives. Using 3D printers, we can already make copies of plastic and metal objects. The next step is to copy living tissue.

Entertainment

Full immersion virtual reality will be with us in perhaps ten to twenty years' time. We will be able to plant tiny microchips in the brain, allowing a person to experience games, movies, and virtual life as if they are real. As computers interact with the brain, we will have the sensation of touching, seeing, hearing, and smelling virtual objects in virtual worlds. Instead of just watching heroes in movies, signals to the brain will let us feel what our heroes feel, see what they see. Fortunately, if things get too terrifying, we will be able to switch it off with the push of a button!

Global problems

In the next thirty years, climate change is going to seriously affect traditional farming. Floods and droughts will disrupt farming patterns that have existed for thousands of years. Because of this, cities will have to start producing food, and vertical farming will become common. Tower blocks and skyscrapers will have gardens built into them. Each floor will grow different plants, fruits and vegetables, and the water will be recycled. Instead of stretching out for miles across the landscape, farmland will now rise hundreds of meters into the air.

VOCABULARY

FUTURE TIME MARKERS

3 A Read sentences 1–6 from the article in Exercise 2A and underline the time markers.

1 <u>In the near future</u>, we may be able to communicate in any language we choose.
2 <u>In only a year or two</u> the machine, which will be a headset, could come onto the market …
3 Another big development probably won't be ready <u>in the short term</u>,
4 … <u>in the long term</u> there is hope that 3D printers will make copies of body parts …
5 Full immersion virtual reality will be with us <u>in perhaps ten to twenty years' time</u>.
6 <u>In the next thirty years</u>, climate change is going to seriously affect traditional farming.

B Look at the time markers again. Which of them mean *soon*? Which mean *in a long time*? Which name a future date or time period? Group them.

C ▶ 3.3 **STRESS IN TIME MARKERS** Listen to the underlined expressions in 3A. Which words in these expressions are stressed? Which words are the most important to the meaning of each expression?

D Work in pairs. Ask and answer the questions using both the time markers given.

1 Will you still live in the same place: a) in the near future? b) in ten years' time?
2 What projects will you work on: a) in the short term? b) in the long term?
3 Will your working life/life as a student change: a) in the next five to ten years? b) in a year or two?

GRAMMAR

THE FUTURE (PREDICTIONS)

4 A Read the extracts from the article. Are the predictions certain (C) or possible (P)?

1 We <u>may</u> be able to communicate in any language we choose. *P*
2 In only a year or two, the headset <u>could</u> come onto the market.
3 This <u>is likely to</u> save millions of lives.
4 Climate change <u>is going to</u> seriously affect traditional farming.
5 Tower blocks and skyscrapers <u>will</u> have gardens.

B Look at the underlined words above. Complete the rules with *will*, *could*, *to* or *be*.

> **RULES**
>
> 1 We use ___*will*___ + infinitive without *to* to make predictions about the future.
> 2 We use _____ *going to* + infinitive without *to* to make predictions when there is present evidence.
> 3 We use *may* or _____ + infinitive without *to* to say something is possible but not certain.
> 4 We use *likely* + infinitive with _____ to say something will probably happen.

▷ page 72 **LANGUAGEBANK**

5 A Circle the correct alternative to complete the text.

Dr Michio Kaku is a physicist who makes TV programmes about the future. He believes we [1]*will be design/will design* new worlds that look like our own, and that virtual reality is [2]*become/going to become* more like our reality. In one programme, Kaku jumps into a remote controlled car, and tells us the car is so intelligent that the words 'traffic jam' and 'traffic accident' [3]*are going to diappear/going to disappear* from the language. He also says that in a few years' time microchips will be so cheap they [4]*are could be built/could be built* into every product we buy – our walls, our furniture, even our clothes. And they [5]*likely/are likely* to be so small we [6]*won't know/won't to know* they exist. Kaku also believes our sunglasses [7]*may become/may becoming* our future home entertainment centre. He then does a virtual dance using 3-D technology (his dance partner is hundreds of miles away) and explains that one day in the near future, 3-D technology [8]*is could replace/could replace* the telephone and [9]*reduce might/might reduce* air travel. Finally, he investigates robots and concludes that, in the long term, some of our closest friends [10]*might not be/might be not* people.

B Discuss. Which predictions, if they come true, will be good/bad for the world? Why?

SPEAKING

6 A Look at the pictures about the world in 2040. What information did you already know? Is there anything you find surprising or unlikely?

B Imagine you are a 'futurist' and it's your job to predict the future. Think about the topics in the box. What changes do you think will happen in these areas by 2040? Make some notes.

> communication   technology   food
> work habits   cities   the environment

C Work in pairs and discuss your ideas.

Communication: I think we will probably have video conference calls with people's holograms. There probably won't be …

THE WORLD IN 2040

9 BILLION

INDIA **CHINA**

ENERGY green energy dominates: solar and wind power; no coal; no nuclear plants

HEALTH AIDS eradicated; old cancers now curable, new forms of cancer incurable

POPULATION 9 billion; India overtakes China as most populous country

EDUCATION 70% literacy

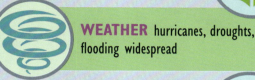

WEATHER hurricanes, droughts, flooding widespread

TRANSPORT AND TRAVEL hydrogen-fuelled transport, electric cars common in developed countries; self-driving cars; hotel opens on The Moon; first tourists go to Mars

POLITICS several countries cease to exist — 30% of island nations submerged under water; United States of Europe a global superpower to rival China

VOCABULARY *PLUS*

IDIOMS

7 A Read comments 1–4. Which of the topics in the images are they referring to?

1 'I like that statistic. I teach reading, so it's an issue that's <u>close to my heart</u>.'

2 'If that statistic is correct, then coastal countries like mine are running out of time.'

3 'This hits the nail on the head: we will eradicate old illnesses, but new ones will develop.'

4 'Let's face it: the world will be completely overcrowded.'

B Read the definition of an idiom and underline the idioms in sentences 1–4.

> **idiom** /ˈɪdɪəm/ [C] a group of words that have a special meaning when they are used together: '*On top of the world*' is an idiom meaning '*very happy*'

From Longman Active Study Dictionary.

C Look at the underlined idioms in Exercise 7A and decide if these statements about idioms are true (T) or false (F)?

1 Idioms are usually formal.

2 You cannot usually change the order of words in an idiom.

3 You can sometimes change the verb tense and the subject of an idiom.

4 You can usually guess the meaning from one word in the idiom.

D Work in pairs and compare your answers. Then turn to page 84 to check your answers.

Then turn to page 84

speakout TIP

Write new idioms in a special place in your vocabulary notebook. Record them in context and add your own examples. Do this for the idioms in Exercises 7 and 8A. Then try them out. Make sure it's the right situation and you use the exact words.

8 Work in pairs. Look at the idioms organised by topic. What do the underlined idioms mean?

Problems

1 We forgot to pay our taxes. Now we're <u>in hot water</u>.

2 I said the wrong thing again. I always <u>put my foot in it</u>.

Time

3 We're <u>working against the clock</u>. We have two hours to finish the project.

4 I'm sure we can win this match but we're <u>running out of time</u>.

9 Look at the idioms organised by key words. Match idioms 1–6 with meanings a)–f).

Body parts

1 Keep an eye on him. *b*

2 Can you give me a hand?

Food and drink

3 It's not my cup of tea.

4 It was a piece of cake.

Animals

5 You're a dark horse!

6 I want to get out of the rat race.

a) I don't like it

b) watch

c) help me

d) the competitive world of work

e) you have a lot of secrets

f) easy

10 A Find and correct the mistakes. There is a mistake in each sentence.

1 When was the last time you gave someone the hand?

2 Which student do you think is a horse dark?

3 When's the last time you put your feet in it?

4 Which issues are close by your heart?

5 Do you often have to work against the clocks?

6 When were you last in warm water?

B Write an answer to each question. Then compare your answers.

▷ page 80 **VOCABULARY**BANK

page 80 VOCABULARYBANK

F dealing with misunderstandings
P linking in connected speech
V misunderstandings

VOCABULARY
MISUNDERSTANDINGS

1 Look at the photos. What is the situation in each one?

2 A Read sentences 1–8 and complete them with phrases a)–h). Which are about future arrangements?

1 When we meet later, make sure you go to the Judd Road in the town centre because …
2 We mistakenly left home at 5.30 because …
3 I was expecting to see Pete, my old school friend, but …
4 I didn't do the homework because …
5 I organised a party for tomorrow night! I thought her birthday was 6th May but …
6 I ended up at the wrong house because …
7 I called Deb to invite her over, but she thought I was a stranger because …
8 I answered the phone, but …

a) it was a **wrong number**.
b) I'd got the **wrong address**.
c) we **got the date wrong**.
d) **we thought** it started at 6.
e) **it was a different** Peter Smith.
f) there are two streets **with the same name**.
g) she **didn't recognise** my voice.
h) I **didn't realise** it was for today.

B Which expressions in bold show misunderstandings about: a) people b) places c) times d) someone on the phone?

C Can you remember a misunderstanding in your life about a time, person, place, etc? What happened? Tell other students.

FUNCTION
DEALING WITH MISUNDERSTANDINGS

3 A ▶ 3.4 Listen to four telephone conversations involving misunderstandings. What was the misunderstanding in each conversation?

B Listen again and answer the questions.

Conversation 1
1 Who did the woman want to speak to?
2 Who did she speak to?

Conversation 2
3 How did David make his hotel reservation?
4 What hotel does he want to stay in?

Conversation 3
5 What time does the show finish?
6 What time did the show start?

Conversation 4
7 What does the woman want to rent?
8 What is the date?

C Complete expressions 1–7 with the words in the box.

tell   that   me (x2)   saying   mean   name   again

1 I didn't catch any of _____.
2 You've lost _____.
3 Could you repeat the last _____?
4 Can you say that _____?
5 What exactly do you _____?
6 I don't get what you're _____.
7 Do you mean to _____ _____ … ?

D ▶ 3.5 Listen and check. Then listen again and copy the intonation.

▷ page 68 **LANGUAGE**BANK

4 A Put the underlined words in the correct order to complete B's responses. Use capital letters where necessary.

1 **A:** Oh no! I can't find the key.
  B: do say mean to you we're going to be locked out all night?
  Do you mean to say

2 **A:** And after Jimmy left Minnie, he married Millie, who used to be married to Billy.
  B: lost me you've. Who are all these people?

3 **A:** There was a little accident with the spaghetti bolognese and your sofa.
  B: mean exactly what you do?

4 **A:** The boss wants to see you. It's about the money that's missing from the accounts.
  B: what don't saying get you're I.

5 **A:** Um, er, I think my new phone number is, um, 654 0987 6743.
  B: catch I that any of didn't. What's the number?

6 **A:** My home address is 39 Kings Street, Manchester, Lancashire, M8 2TO.
  B: that you say again can? I didn't hear.

7 **A:** We're leaving Los Angeles at 11p.m. OK? Then we arrive in Sydney at 5.50a.m.
  B: part you the repeat could last? I didn't hear you.

B Work in pairs. What does speaker A say next? Continue the conversations with your own words.

LEARN TO

REFORMULATE

5 A Read the extracts from audio 3.4. Underline five examples of how the speaker reformulates what he/she heard.

1 **A:** We've got no reservations in the name of Cullinan, and we're fully booked tonight.
  B: So you're saying I can't stay here. This is the Sheldon Hotel, yes?

2 **C:** Didn't you say it starts at seven?
  D: No, it starts at five and finishes at seven!
  C: So what you mean is I've missed the whole show.

3 **E:** Yes, but today's a holiday and all the cars have been booked already.
  F: Do you mean to tell me that there's nothing at all? No cars available?
  E: There's nothing till tomorrow, I'm afraid.
  F: But I definitely booked a car for today, the third of July.
  E: It's the fourth of July today. In other words, your booking was for yesterday.

B ▶ **3.6** **LINKING IN CONNECTED SPEECH** Listen to the phrases. Notice how the words are linked together in fast speech.

So you're saying …

C Listen again and repeat the phrases.

SPEAKING

6 A Work in pairs and role-play the situation.

Student A

You are a guest at a hotel. Twenty minutes ago you called reception, asking for some soap to be sent to your room. Room service brought you some tomato soup. You want them to take the soup back and bring some soap. Call reception to make your complaint.

Student B

You are a receptionist at a hotel. A guest calls to make a complaint. Start the conversation by saying 'Reception. How can I help you?'

Hello. Yes, I'm afraid I have a problem … Explain the problem.

Apologise for the misunderstanding and say you will send someone with soap.

Check details and thank the receptionist for their help.

Confirm details, apologise again and end the call.

B Change roles and turn to page 84.

C Work in pairs and take turns. Student A: ring reception and make a complaint. Student B: apologise and offer a solution. Use the flow charts to help and role-play the situations.

DVD PREVIEW

1 A Read six opinions about YouTube. What do the words in bold mean?

1 I love YouTube because the **creators** of the videos are often normal people like us, the **consumers**.

2 The thing I hate about YouTube is the **adverts**, especially when you can't skip them.

3 The **audience** for some YouTube videos may be bigger than for some TV programmes.

4 Most of the **content** on YouTube is terrible. The filming **techniques** are low quality.

5 I don't go on YouTube that much and I'd never **subscribe** to a YouTube channel.

6 Making good quality YouTube videos requires a big **investment** of time and money.

B Work in pairs and discuss statements 1–6 above. Which ones do you agree with?

2 Read the programme information. What is it about? Who does the presenter speak to?

▶)) The Culture Show YouTube: The Future of TV?

BBC

This BBC documentary looks at the rise of YouTube and finds out what the company is doing to improve its online content. Jacques Peretti goes into the YouTube office and talks to some of the young creators who are changing the entertainment industry.

DVD VIEW

3 Watch the DVD. What is YouTube doing to improve its online content?

4 A Watch the DVD again and complete the fact file.

VALUE:	$1,000,000,000
FOUNDED:	in ¹_____ .
CREATORS:	for some, YouTube is a full-time job
MAKING MONEY:	YouTube invites popular creators to put ²_____ on their videos.
STUDIO:	creators with 50,000 ³_____ can use the studio.
BIGGEST STUDIO:	'Deep Focus'
CRITICISM OF BUSINESS MODEL:	⁴_____ think content should be free.

B Work in pairs. Answer the questions.

1 Who has 'some of the biggest audiences in Britain'?

2 Who makes more money: YouTube video creators or TV programme makers?

3 What kind of techniques do creators learn in the YouTube studios?

4 What will 'a better quality of content' bring for YouTube?

5 What does Andrew Keen say about the internet and 'the creative community'?

C Watch the DVD again to check your answers.

5 Discuss in groups.

1 Do you think the DVD clip is positive or negative about YouTube, or is it balanced?

2 What do you think of the type of short clips ('kids messing around in their bedrooms') in the programme?

3 Do you think that YouTube is 'the future of TV'? Do you think it will become more popular than mainstream TV or is it only aimed at young people?

speakout create a video channel

6 A You are going to create your own video channel. Think about the points below. Is there any other important information you should consider?

- name of channel
- type of video clips
- target audience
- what's special about the channel
- who will star in the videos
- competitors/rivals
- how frequently you will upload new videos

B ▶ **3.7** Listen to two people planning a new YouTube channel. What do they say about each of the points in Exercise 6A?

C Listen again and tick the key phrases you hear.

> **KEY PHRASES**
>
> The first thing [I think] is …
> We came up with this idea.
> It would be really [cool/interesting/fun] to …
> What's the angle?
> So the target audience is …
> Who will be the presenters?
> Who are our competitors or rivals?
> How often will we upload new videos?
> What about a name?

7 A Work in groups. Think of an idea for the task in Exercise 6A. Make sure you discuss all the points and take notes.

B Work with another group and take turns to present your ideas. What are the advantages and disadvantages of each idea?

writeback a proposal

8 A A new company is looking for funding to make videos. Read the company's proposal. Do you think it will get funding? Why?/Why not?

FUTURE SHOCK VIDEOS

We are looking for funding to make exciting and innovative videos about a topic that is close to everyone's heart: the environment. In the long term there will be big changes to the natural world including floods and major earthquakes. As a group of environmental scientists, we intend to predict the effects of these changes and, ultimately, to help prevent them.

We will combine straight reporting, docudrama and science fiction. The videos will be presented by some of the nation's leading scientists and thinkers, as well as actors. We will upload new videos once a month.

Our target audience is anyone interested in how the world will look in the next 30–100 years. It could be other scientists, students or anyone from the general public.

We thank you for your attention and look forward to hearing from you soon.

James Toffler

Please see the attachment for funding scales and further details of our financial plan.

B Use the sentence openers below to write a proposal for your idea from Exercise 7A. Invent any additional details you want to.

We are looking for …
We intend to …
The videos will be presented by …
We will upload new videos …
Our target audience is …
We thank you for …

C Work with a different group from the one you worked with in Exercise 7B and exchange proposals. Do you think the other group's proposal is worth funding? Why?/Why not?

V ORGANISATION

1 A Complete the sentences with words from the box.

wisely ahead minute time prioritise multitask off
distracted done started deadline

1 It's late. I really think we should get _____.
2 Why do you always have to leave things until the last _____?
3 Sorry, I got _____ by the football on the television.
4 You've got so many things to do. You'll have to _____ and start with the most important.
5 I worked hard and got a lot of things _____ this morning.
6 I'm afraid they're just wasting your _____.
7 I'd like to get this done _____ of time, so we can go on holiday.
8 I keep putting _____ writing my essay.
9 I'm going to have to stay up all night or I'll never meet the _____ for this work.
10 We won't be here for long, so use your time _____.
11 I think it's better not to _____ but to focus on doing one job at a time.

B Work in pairs. Choose two or three of the phrases from Exercise 1A and use them to make short dialogues.

A: We need to get a lot of things done, but we don't have much time.
B: Right. We'd better get started.

G THE FUTURE (PLANS)

2 A Complete the paragraphs with phrases from the box.

'm going to have having 'm organising might 'm finishing
are going I'll be are coming will going to

I [1]_____ work at the end of the month. I've been a teacher here for nearly twenty years, so [2]_____ sad when I leave the school for the last time. But in the future, I [3]_____ more time to do some of the things I enjoy. My wife and I [4]_____ travelling. We [5]_____ visit Australia, which I've always wanted to do.

I'm [6]_____ be forty next month, so I'm [7]_____ a big party. Lots of people [8]_____ that I don't see very often, so I'm really looking forward to it. I [9]_____ a band, and lots of delicious food and drink, so everyone [10]_____ have a good time.

B Write a short paragraph describing a plan you have for the future. Then compare your ideas with a partner.

V FUTURE TIME MARKERS

3 A Choose the correct ending in each case, a) b) or c).

1 I might live in *a foreign country* in the long a) time b) term c) days.
2 I hope to *be retired* in twenty years' a) future b) ahead c) time.
3 I will finish *this course* in a month a) or two b) coming c) time.
4 I hope to *write my autobiography* a long time a) ago b) ahead c) from now.
5 I want to buy *a new car* in the near a) time b) future c) term.
6 I'm going to *go travelling* next a) year b) years c) future.

B Choose four of the sentences above. Change the words in italics so they are true for you.

G THE FUTURE (PREDICTIONS)

4 A Find and correct the grammatical mistakes. One sentence is correct.

1 Man not will fly for fifty years. (1901)
2 There isn't going be any German reunification this century. (1984)
3 Democracy will to be dead by 1950. (1936)
4 By 1980 all power (electric, atomic, solar) is likely be almost free. (1956)
5 The Japanese car industry isn't likely to be successful in the US market. (1968)
6 Man will be never reach the Moon. (1957)
7 Television won't very matter in your lifetime or mine. (1936)
8 The internet may to become useful for business but never for the general public. (1989)

B Change the verbs so they mean the opposite and become intelligent predictions. You may need to change some other words.

Man will fly within fifty years

F DEALING WITH MISUNDERSTANDINGS

5 A Complete B's responses using the words in the box.

lost mean to say saying
don't do

1 **A:** I've heard that a lot of our employees like you.
   B: I [1]_____ get what you're [2]_____.
   A: And I'm looking for someone to take over the business when I retire.
   B: What exactly [3]_____ you [4]_____?

2 **A:** David Johnson and Johnny Thomson are going to meet Tommy Davies tonight.
   B: You've [5]_____ me.
   A: Johnson, Thomson and Davies are the company directors. They're meeting to discuss the company's future.
   B: Do you mean [6]_____ [7]_____ they're meeting without me?

B Work in pairs. Write a dialogue that uses three of the phrases in Exercise 5A. Act out your dialogues.

4 jobs

MILLIONAIRES p44

DREAM JOB p47

THAT'S A GOOD IDEA p50

BBC

Good Luck!

GAVIN AND STACEY p52

BBC
INTERVIEWS

Is your job a 'dream job'?

G must/have to/should
P fast speech: *have to*
V personal qualities; confusing words

VOCABULARY

PERSONAL QUALITIES

1 A Read about the qualities people need to do their jobs. Which jobs do you think they are talking about?

❝ Winning is the most important thing for me. I've always been **competitive**, so I love my job. I think I'm **a good leader**. It's important that all the players know what they're doing and it's my job to tell them. The decisions I make are important for the whole team, so I can't be **indecisive**. ❞

❝ I have classes of 80 to 100 children so I have to be **hard-working**. I do my best, because education is so important for the children. You need to be **a good communicator** in my job, so that you can get the children interested in what they have to learn. Often, we don't have very many resources, so we also need to be creative and be able to **think outside the box**. ❞

❝ I'm **a risk taker**, so starting my own business wasn't difficult for me. I've always been very **motivated** and **ambitious**. I start work at 4.30a.m. every day. I don't enjoy sleep. You can't afford to be lazy if you want to make money. ❞

B Match the words and phrases in bold above with the definitions 1–9.

1 work with a lot of effort _____
2 have problems making a decision _____
3 think differently or in a new way _____
4 want to be more successful than others _____
5 want to be successful or powerful _____
6 want to achieve somethng because it's interesting or exciting _____
7 person who does things which are dangerous _____
8 person who has the qualities to manage a group of people _____
9 person who can express ideas or feelings clearly to others _____

C Which qualities do you think you have? Work in pairs and compare your answers.

▷ page 81 **VOCABULARY**BANK

READING

2 A Which of the personal qualities discussed in Exercise 1 do you think are qualities you need to become a millionaire?

B Are the statements 1–6 about millionaires true (T) or false (F)?

1 Most millionaires are born rich.
2 Millionaires think that money is more important than love or marriage.
3 They work more than sixty hours a week.
4 They don't like to work when they're on holiday.
5 They do well at school and usually go to university.
6 They like spending money on designer goods.

C Read the article and check your answers.

D Work in pairs. Do you agree with the article? Do any of the facts surprise you? Why?

"You don't have to be born rich to be a millionaire"

1 So you want to be a millionaire, but have you got what it takes? To find out what millionaires are really like and what motivates them, the BBC programme *Mind of a Millionaire* did a survey. Psychologists looked at self-made millionaires to try and understand what qualities are needed to make a million. So, what is really important to a millionaire?

2 The answer, not surprisingly, is money, money and more money. Money is more important than love or marriage. And if you give a millionaire money, they won't spend it, they'll invest it to make more money. But you don't have to be born rich to be a millionaire. Most millionaires come from relatively poor backgrounds. And you don't have to work hard at school either. A lot of successful entrepreneurs were lazy at school and didn't get good results. However, you must have a clear idea of what you want to do (get rich) and you really ought to start early. A lot of millionaires left school early, to start their own businesses.

3 **A** Underline words or phrases in the article that match meanings 1–6.

1 their family didn't have much money (paragraph 2)
2 they never stop thinking about work (paragraph 3)
3 having enough time for work and for the things you enjoy (paragraph 3)
4 work long hours (paragraph 3)
5 find something for a good price (paragraph 5)
6 do what you want without worrying about what other people think (paragraph 5)

B Work in pairs. Choose two or three of the expressions. Use them to make sentences about yourself, or people you know.

GRAMMAR

MUST/HAVE TO/SHOULD (OBLIGATION)

4 **A** Match the words in bold in sentences 1–6 with the meanings a)–e). One meaning matches with two sentences.

1 You **don't have to** be born rich to be a millionaire.
2 If you want to be a millionaire, you **have to** work hard.
3 You **must** have a clear idea of what you want to do.
4 You **should** enjoy your work.
5 You **shouldn't** take too many holidays.
6 You **mustn't** worry about what other people think of you.

a) It's a good idea.
b) It's not necessary. You don't need to be/do this.
c) It's necessary. You have no choice.
d) It's important that you don't do this.
e) It's not a good idea.

B ▶ **4.1** **FAST SPEECH: *have to*** Listen to the pronunciation of *have to* /hæftə/ in fast speech. Listen and repeat the sentences.

▷ page 74 **LANGUAGE**BANK

5 **A** Make sentences with the prompts. Use the positive or negative form of the word in brackets.

1 postmen / get up early in the morning (have)
Postmen have to get up early in the morning.
2 window cleaners / be afraid of heights (must)
3 nurses / be patient and care about other people (should)
4 businessmen often / travel a lot (have)
5 politicians / do their job because they want fame (should)
6 teachers / enjoy working with children (must)
7 doctors / train for several years before they can work (have)
8 teachers / work in the school during the holidays (have)
9 police officers / good communicators / be (have)

▷ page 81 **VOCABULARY**BANK

B Work in pairs. Think about three different jobs. Make sentences to describe what qualities are/aren't important for these jobs. Read your sentences to your partner. Can they guess which job it is?

A: *These people have to be motivated. They should be good communicators, especially when talking to children. And they have to be very patient.*
B: *Teachers?*

3 If you want to be a millionaire, not only do you have to work hard, but you should enjoy your work. And you shouldn't take too many holidays. Most millionaires work more than sixty hours a week. Half stay in contact with the office while they're on holiday and fourteen percent of them refuse to switch off. Having a good work-life balance is fine for people who only want to be moderately successful, but if you're really ambitious, you have to put in the hours.

4 What are millionaires like as people? The survey found that they are competitive, they like taking risks, and they are aggressive and self-confident. They'll do anything they can to get what they want.

5 Millionaires can break all sorts of rules. The only thing they mustn't do is break the law. Surprisingly, most millionaires are careful spenders. They prefer Gap to Gucci. Many of them choose not to spend money on expensive designer clothes – they would rather find a bargain on the high street. And they don't spend lots of money on expensive meals in restaurants either. They prefer to eat at home. However, they do like to drive Mercedes and go on at least three expensive holidays a year. One last thing: millionaires don't care what other people think of them. So, if you want to be a millionaire, you shouldn't worry about what other people think of you. Just do your own thing.

SPEAKING

6 A Work in pairs. Do the quiz. Then check your score on page 85.

B Discuss. How many of the questions did you answer like a millionaire? Do you agree with the results on page 85? Is getting rich something which concerns you? Why?/Why not?

VOCABULARY PLUS
CONFUSING WORDS

7 Read the vocabulary notes and complete sentences 1 and 2.

> **job • work**
>
> **Work** is what you do to earn money:
> *What kind of **work** does he do?*
>
> A **job** is the particular type of work that you do:
> *Sam's got a **job** as a waiter.*
>
> **Job** can be plural, but **work** cannot.

1 I've finished my degree, so I'm looking for a _____.
2 It's not easy to find _____ when you're my age.

8 A Underline the correct alternative in the sentences below. What is the difference between these words?

1 He suddenly *remembered/reminded* that he had to go to the bank.
2 I have to call my boss later. Can you *remember/remind* me?
3 I've *forgotten/left* my keys in the car. I really should get them.
4 Did you *hear/listen* that noise?
5 Can you say that again? I'm sorry, I wasn't *listening/hearing*.
6 Being ill on holiday isn't much *fun/funny*.

B Turn to page 160 to check your answers.

▷ page 81 **VOCABULARY**BANK

speakout TIP

To help you remember confusing words and vocabulary, write them in personalised sentences in your notebook. Write sentences about your life using some of the words from Exercise 8.

9 A Complete questions 1–6 with a suitable word from Exercises 7 and 8.

1 What are the best paid _____ in your country?
2 Is there anything you often _____, like phone numbers or someone's name?
3 If you _____ carefully, what noises can you hear at the moment?
4 Do you write notes to _____ yourself about important things?
5 How much did you _____ for your first job? What did you buy?
6 What do you like doing for _____? Do you like playing games?

B Work in pairs. Take turns to ask and answer the questions above.

HAVE YOU GOT WHAT IT TAKES TO BE A MILLIONAIRE?

Do you answer these questions like a millionaire would?

1 Would you like to be …
- a) a bit richer
- b) a lot richer
- c) mega rich

2 If you wanted a pair of shoes that you couldn't afford, would you …
- a) buy them anyway
- b) wait until the sales and risk losing them
- c) walk away

3 How many credit cards do you carry with you?
- a) One or none
- b) Two
- c) More than two

4 If you could just afford to pay for it, would you splash out on …
- a) a heated swimming pool
- b) a racehorse
- c) a big party for all your friends

5 Do you most enjoy stories about …
- a) romance
- b) adventure
- c) mystery

6 Do you check that your bill is correct after a meal out?
- a) Yes
- b) No
- c) Only if I'm alone

7 What is 9 multiplied by 8?
- a) Did you get the answer right instantly?
- b) Or only after doing little sums in your head?
- c) Did you get the wrong answer?

8 If a favourite relative left you a watch that was not your style, would you …
- a) sell it
- b) keep it to sell on a rainy day
- c) keep it to help you remember them

DREAM JOB

G used to, would
P intonation: emphasis; linking: *used to*
V extreme adjectives

LISTENING

1 Work in pairs. Look at the photos and answer the questions.

1 What are these jobs? Would you like to do them? Why?/Why not?

2 What is your idea of a dream job?

2 A ▶ **4.2** Listen to people talking about their dream jobs. Match the speaker to the photos.

B What problem does each speaker talk about?

C Listen again and answer questions 1–8. Write Nicola (N), Luca (L) or Amy (A).

1 Who had a boss who worked in the media?

2 Who worked for a big company?

3 Who spent a lot of time by the sea as a child?

4 Who had to try and invent new ideas for the job?

5 Who decided to do this job because they saw someone else doing it?

6 Who had a different job in the summer and in the winter?

7 Who had a difficult relationship with their boss?

8 Who started to find their job boring?

D Check your answers by reading audio script 4.2 on page 90.

VOCABULARY

EXTREME ADJECTIVES

3 Find the extreme adjectives in bold in audio script 4.2 on page 90. Match them to the gradable adjectives below.

1 good: wonderful, amazing, _____
2 bad: awful, _____
3 big: enormous
4 small: tiny
5 tasty: _____
6 hot: _____

7 cold: freezing
8 tired: exhausted
9 angry: _____
10 interesting: _____
11 pretty: _____
12 difficult: _____

4 A Complete conversations 1–6 with extreme adjectives.

1 **A:** The food here tastes so good.
   B: Yes, it's _____.

2 **A:** It's over thirty degrees outside today.
   B: I know. It's absolutely _____.

3 **A:** Was your girlfriend angry about you being late?
   B: Yes, she was really _____.

4 **A:** The view of the lake is really pretty.
   B: Yes, it's _____, isn't it?

5 **A:** Do you find the job interesting?
   B: I think it's absolutely _____.

6 **A:** It's hard to understand what he's saying.
   B: I know. It's _____.

B ▶ **4.3** **INTONATION: emphasis** Listen and mark the stress on the adjectives. Notice how speaker B emphasises the stressed syllable in their intonation.

C Listen again and shadow speaker B's response.

A Amy

B Nicola

C Luca

GRAMMAR
USED TO, WOULD

5 A Read the texts. What did the children dream of doing? Have they achieved their dreams?

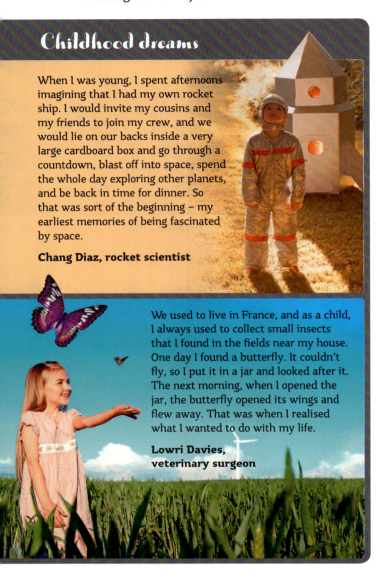

Childhood dreams

When I was young, I spent afternoons imagining that I had my own rocket ship. I would invite my cousins and my friends to join my crew, and we would lie on our backs inside a very large cardboard box and go through a countdown, blast off into space, spend the whole day exploring other planets, and be back in time for dinner. So that was sort of the beginning – my earliest memories of being fascinated by space.

Chang Diaz, rocket scientist

We used to live in France, and as a child, I always used to collect small insects that I found in the fields near my house. One day I found a butterfly. It couldn't fly, so I put it in a jar and looked after it. The next morning, when I opened the jar, the butterfly opened its wings and flew away. That was when I realised what I wanted to do with my life.

Lowri Davies, veterinary surgeon

B Look at the underlined words in sentences a)–d) and match them with rules 1–3.

a) I would invite my cousins and my friends to join my crew.

b) We used to live in France.

c) I always used to collect small insects.

d) One day I found a butterfly.

> **RULES**
> **1** Use the past simple, not *used to* or *would,* to talk about specific events in the past. _____
> **2** Use *used to* or *would* to talk about a past habit. You can also use the past simple. _____ and _____
> **3** Use *used to* to talk about a past state. You cannot use *would* to talk about a past state. _____

▷ page 74 **LANGUAGE**BANK

6 A Complete the texts. Where possible, use *would*. Where neither *used to* or *would* are possible, use the past simple.

> It's every young girl's dream to be an actress when she grows up. I ¹_____ (love) watching beautiful actresses on television. I was so sure that was what I wanted to do that I ²_____ (practise) my Oscar speech in front of the mirror in the bathroom. I ³_____ (use) a shampoo bottle instead of a microphone, and I ⁴_____ (thank) all my family and friends, even my three cats, for helping me!

> My family ⁵_____ (live) in Sheffield, just near the football stadium, so as a child, I ⁶_____ (go) to football matches most weekends. I remember the first match I went to, my granddad ⁷_____ (take) me. I was very young, and I had never seen so many people in one place at one time. It was quite frightening, and I don't think I ⁸_____ (watch) the game very much. But I remember that we won, and the crowd went crazy. After that, every week I ⁹_____ (ask) Granddad if he had tickets, and usually he did.

B ▶ **4.4** **LINKING:** *used to* Listen and repeat. Notice the pronunciation of *used to* /juːstə/. Practise saying the sentences.

1 I used to play football when I was a kid.
2 I used to practise every day.
3 We used to live in London.
4 I didn't use to like classical music.
5 My father used to take me fishing.
6 I used to ski, but now I snowboard.
7 We used to go to the cinema a lot.

C Did you use to do any of the things mentioned above? Tell your partner.

SPEAKING

7 Work in pairs and discuss.

1 What were your childhood dreams? Have you achieved them?

2 Did you have any interests or hobbies in the past which relate to your life (job/studies) now? What were they?

3 How have your ideas, opinions, hobbies, etc., changed? (Think about food you liked/hated as a child, television programmes you enjoyed etc.) Are there any things that you used to do, which you don't do now? Why did you stop? Would you do these things again?

As a child, I always used to dream about being an artist …

WRITING

A COVERING LETTER; LEARN TO ORGANISE YOUR IDEAS

8 Read the text below and answer the questions.

1 What kind of person would be good at this job?

2 Would you like to do this job? Why?/Why not?

> Would you like to travel the world staying in some of the world's top holiday resorts for free? A luxury travel company is looking for a reviewer to try out top hotels and holiday resorts for one year. The lucky applicant will be expected to stay in a variety of locations that include Caribbean islands, waterside hotels in Venice, and some of the world's top ski destinations, as well as Las Vegas and Buenos Aires. They will be expected to write about their experiences on the company blog. No formal qualifications are needed. However, the successful applicant will be sociable, have great communication skills and, of course, a passion for travel.

9 A Read the covering letter. Do you think this person would be good for the job? Why?/Why not?

---

1 Dear Matthew Ray,

2 I'm writing to you regarding your advertisement for a professional travel reviewer which I saw on www.findajob.com. I would like to submit an application for the position. Please find my CV attached.

3 As an experienced travel blogger who has spent the last five years travelling around the world, I believe that I meet all the requirements you outline in your advertisement.

Good communicator with excellent language skills: As a regular travel blogger, over the last few years, I have built and maintained a wide audience of readers. I have also published newspaper and magazine articles and given radio interviews about my travel experiences. I am fluent in English and French, and also speak a little Russian.

Interest in travel and tourism: In addition to my own travels, I worked for six months for a tour bus company in Australia, where I had hands-on experience of tour guiding.

Proven ability in website management: As well as maintaining my own website, consisting of a journal and video weblog, with up-to-date photos and stories of my travels, I have helped to manage the website for a youth hostel in Ireland.

4 If you require any further information, or would like to arrange an interview, please call me on 07788658429 or email me at mjdaley@yahoo.com. I look forward to hearing from you at your earliest convenience.

5 Yours sincerely,

Megan Daley

B Is the wording of the letter formal or informal? Find examples of expressions which tell you this.

C Underline phrases in the letter which match meanings 1–6.

1 about (paragraph 2)

2 I want to apply for the job (paragraph 2)

3 I think I would be good for the job (paragraph 3)

4 practical experience of doing the job (paragraph 3)

5 I have shown that I am able to do this (paragraph 3)

6 as soon as you have the opportunity (paragraph 4)

D Underline any other useful phrases.

10 Match the parts of the letter 1–5 with notes a)–e).

Preparing a covering letter

A What qualities are they looking for? Write three to four points that show you have these qualities. Use the same words as they use in the advertisement.

B Address your letter to an individual. Only use 'Dear Sir/Madam' when you can't find out the recipient's name.

C Finish with a call to action. What is going to happen next? Are you going to call them or should they call you?

D Explain why you are contacting them. What is the job? Where have you seen it?

E Use 'Yours sincerely' if you know their name or 'Yours faithfully' if you don't

11 Look at the job advertisements on page 86 and write a covering letter for one of the jobs. Use the sample letter and useful phrases to help you.

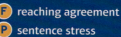

F reaching agreement
P sentence stress
V business

VOCABULARY

BUSINESS

1 A Work in pairs. Discuss. Would you consider starting your own business? What kind of business would you start? Is there anything stopping you from doing it?

B Complete the questions with words from the box.

fired   salary   work   compete   runs   idea   interview   charge

1 Do you know anyone who _____ their own company?
2 Have you ever been in _____ of a team of people?
3 Have you ever been out of _____?
4 When did you last go for a job _____?
5 Have you ever had to _____ with others for a job?
6 Which jobs earn a high _____?
7 What kinds of things does someone have to do to get _____ from their job?
8 Can you think of reasons why a business _____ might fail?

C Take turns to ask and answer the questions above.

FUNCTION

REACHING AGREEMENT

2 ▶ 4.5 Listen to a team having a meeting to decide how to set up a new café business. Write some notes about their decisions.

Setting up a new café:
Type of food?   Name?   Location?

3 A Look at the phrases in the table. Listen to the conversation again and tick any of the phrases you hear.

Giving opinions
I (really) feel that …
The way I see things, …
The way I see it, …
Commenting on other opinions
I (don't) see what you mean.
Exactly!
I'm not sure that I agree, actually. ✓
I'm not sure (that's a good idea).
I'm not sure about that.
I think that's a great idea.
That's a good point.
That sounds good.
That's OK by me.
Suggestions
What about … ? / How about … ?
Let's focus on …
I suggest we think about …
I think we should think about …
How about if we (call it) … ?
Why don't we (call it) … ?

B Check your answers in the audio script on page 90.

▷ page 74 **LANGUAGE**BANK

4 A Put the words in the correct order to make sentences and questions.

1 decide / I / on / name / we / think / a / should

2 good / a / that's / point

3 you / see / mean / what / I

4 suggest / location / the / on / I / focus / we

5 fine / that's / me / by

6 sure / I'm / that / agree / not / I

7 we / about / don't / it / why / think / ?

8 business / a / the / about / what / for / name / ?

B ▶ **4.6** SENTENCE STRESS Listen to the phrases. Which words are stressed?

C Listen again and repeat.

LEARN TO

MANAGE A DISCUSSION

5 A Complete the underlined phrases for managing a discussion.

1 <u>First of</u>　　　　 we need to decide on the location.

2 <u>Let's</u>　　　　 on the ideas we had for the location.

3 So, <u>moving on to the next</u>　　　　, what kind of food are we going to serve?

4 　　　　 <u>recap</u>: a Portuguese café selling cakes and lunches, located near the station.

5 <u>I think we need to come</u>　　　　 to the type of café we're establishing.

6 <u>Let's</u>　　　　 up what we've decided.

B ▶ **4.7** Listen and check your answers.

C Cover up Exercise 5A. Which phrase would you use for these situations?

1 the end of a meeting to go over everything that has been discussed?

2 when you want to discuss the next issue?

3 to review what has been discussed so far?

4 to start a meeting and talk about the first point?

5 to get everybody to talk about the same thing?

6 to return to a point that was discussed previously?

SPEAKING

6 A Read the task and write down some ideas.

SET UP A COMPANY TO PROMOTE TOURISM

You are going to set up a tour company to promote tourism in your town/city/country (or the town/country where you are studying). You need to decide the following:

○ the name and location of the company

○ what type of tours you will organise (themed tours/language tours/sports tours, etc.) and where they will go

○ how you will promote tourism

○ how the company will be different from other tour companies

B Work in groups. Read your roles and come up with a plan for the business. You have five minutes.

Student A: It's your job to keep the meeting focused. Try to cover all the points.

Student B: Make sure you make notes about any decisions which are made. You will be the group's spokesperson and will have to sum up at the end of the meeting.

Student C: Try to come up with as many ideas as possible.

C When you are ready, start the discussion like this.

A: Shall we start? First of all, …

D Tell the other groups about your business plan. Which group do you think has the best plan?

DVD PREVIEW

1 Work in pairs. Answer the questions.

1 Do you enjoy watching comedy programmes? Why?/Why not?
2 Which ones are popular in your country?
3 Which comedy programmes do you enjoy watching?

2 Read about the programme. What type of things do you think Gavin needs to learn on his first day at work? Who do you think he will meet?

Gavin and Stacey
BBC

Gavin and Stacey is a BBC programme about a young couple. Gavin comes from Essex, near London, and Stacey comes from Cardiff, Wales. After a long-distance relationship conducted online and by telephone, they eventually get married and Gavin moves to Wales. In this episode, Gavin starts a new job. On his first day, his family want him to do well and be happy at work.

DVD VIEW

3 A Watch the DVD. What is the main problem Gavin has during his first day at work?

B Match DVD extracts 1–5 to the correct responses a)–e).

1 Mr Davies, good to see you again. *b*
2 Did you get your welcome pack?
3 Ready when you are.
4 Now here's somebody you've not met yet.
5 Parcel for you.

a) Oh, thanks.
b) Please, call me Huw.
c) Hi. Nice to meet you.
d) Yeah, I think so.
e) OK, let's show you around.

4 A Answer the questions.

1 What does Huw, the boss, give Gavin?
2 When does Gavin say he will call his mother?
3 How many phone calls does Gavin receive?
4 What does Uncle Bryn bring for Gavin?
5 What is the message on the balloon? Who do you think sent it to him?

B Watch the DVD again to check.

C Discuss. How do you think Gavin will feel at the end of his first day at work?

speakout a day in the life … | writeback your daily routine

5 A ▶ 4.8 Listen to someone describing a typical day in her life. Do you think she likes her job?

B Read the key phrases below. Complete each phrase by adding one word.

> **KEY PHRASES**
>
> I usually wake up _____ (about) 6.30.
> I have to leave home by 8.30 at the _____.
> The first _____ I do when I get to work/school is …
> In the afternoon I _____ to catch up on …
> I usually [make some deliveries/ do some shopping/ …] on my _____ home.
> I try to be _____ by (about) 7 o'clock.
> I _____ just cook supper and watch some television.

C Listen again to check.

D Prepare to tell other students about a normal day in your life. Write notes about your typical day. What do you have in common?

- hours of work/studying
- tasks you have to do
- people you spend your day with
- problems and challenges
- how you relax
- the best parts of your day

6 A Read about a day in the life of a gym instructor. Is his daily routine similar to yours? How is it different?

I work as a gym instructor in a sports centre. I **get up at** 5a.m. every morning and make a cup of coffee. I can't function until I've had my coffee! I drive to work – it takes about fifteen minutes on a good day – **usually getting there at about** 5.40. **The first thing I do is** switch on the lights and the air conditioning if it's summer (heating if it's winter), and then the radio. We have the radio on all day because our clients like listening to the news and the music. The sports centre opens at 6a.m.

I work in a team of four, although only two of us are ever in the gym at the same time. The instructors all wear sports clothes. **It's important to be** comfortable because we sometimes need to show new clients how to use the machines. Apart from this, **our other tasks are** quite simple: we check that everyone has their membership card when they come in, and we check that the machines are clean and safe.

I have a one-hour break for lunch, and I usually do two more hours after lunch. **I go home at about** 2.30.

The best part of the job is meeting people. Our clients range from eighteen-year-old body builders to eighty-year-olds who come to exercise and chat. I've never had any problems at the sports centre. It's a really nice job, though it doesn't pay very well. In the evenings **I relax by** reading a book and cooking for myself, and I'm usually in bed by 9.30p.m.

Frank Carduna

B Write about a typical day in your life using the sentence starters in bold in the text and the key phrases to help. Try to include two or three pieces of information that make your day different from everybody else's. Alternatively, look at the pictures on page 47. Imagine what a day in the life of this person would be like, and write about it.

Ⓥ PERSONAL QUALITIES

1 Work in pairs. Student A: describe a word/phrase from the box in your own words, starting with *I am/like/enjoy*, etc. Don't say the word/phrase. Student B: listen and try to guess the word or phrase.

> hard-working indecisive
> a risk taker a good leader
> ambitious competitive
> think outside the box
> a good communicator

A: *I enjoy working and want to succeed in what I do.*
B: *You're motivated?*
A: *Correct. Your turn to describe a word.*

Ⓖ MUST/HAVE TO/ SHOULD (OBLIGATION)

2 A Underline the correct alternative to complete the sentences.

1 I *have to/mustn't* call my mother today. It's her birthday.
2 I really *must/mustn't* do more exercise. I'm so unfit.
3 I'm lucky because I *don't have to/shouldn't* get up early in the morning. I'm a student.
4 I think you *should/shouldn't* study harder. Your exam results weren't very good.
5 You *mustn't/should* be afraid of taking risks, or you will never live your dreams.
6 I *shouldn't/don't have to* waste so much time on the computer. I'll never finish my work.

B Complete the sentences so that they are true for you.

1 I have to … this evening.
2 I really must do more …
3 I'm lucky because I don't have to …
4 I think you should … because …
5 You mustn't worry about …
6 I shouldn't waste so much time …

C Compare your ideas in pairs.

Ⓥ EXTREME ADJECTIVES

3 A Replace the underlined words in the sentences below with extreme adjectives in the box.

> brilliant fascinating awful
> exhausted tiny boiling
> impossible delicious furious

1 I'm <u>very tired</u>. I didn't sleep well.
2 Shall we open a window? It's <u>very hot</u> in here.
3 My boss just called. He's <u>very angry</u>.
4 I find phrasal verbs <u>very difficult</u> to remember.
5 The holiday was <u>very good</u>, but the weather was <u>very bad</u>.
6 How can you work in this office? It's <u>very small</u>.
7 I find astronomy <u>very interesting</u>.
8 Did you cook this? It's <u>very tasty</u>.

B Work in pairs and take turns to test each other.

A: *Very big.*
B: *Enormous.*
A: *Correct. Your turn.*

Ⓖ USED TO, WOULD

4 A Replace the past simple with *used to* or *would* where possible. Where both are possible, choose *would*.

1 My family lived in Paris, but we moved when I was a teenager.
2 I spent a lot of time with my grandparents when I was younger.
3 For my first job, I washed dishes in a restaurant.
4 I didn't think money was important. Now I have lots of bills to pay.
5 We had a lot more free time before we had children.
6 My best friend at school lived just across the road from me.

B Change four of the sentences so that they are true for you.

C Compare with a partner. Find three things that you both used to do as children, but you don't do now.

Ⓕ REACHING AGREEMENT

5 A Complete the conversations.

1 **A:** The way I s_____ things, all cars should be banned from city centres.
   B: E_____.
2 **A:** I really f_____ that we need to look at immigration.
   B: That's a good p_____
3 **A:** The w_____ I see it, the company is making too much money.
   B: I don't see what you m_____.
4 **A:** I th_____ we should ask for more money.
   B: I'm not s_____ I agree, actually.
5 **A:** I s_____ we try to meet again next week.
   B: T_____ fine by me.

B Work in pairs and practise the conversations.

6 Work in groups. Look at the questions below and discuss. Try to reach agreement on each answer.

> **1** Should there be a limit to the number of hours people can work in one week?

> **2** Should there be a minimum wage? What should it be?

> **3** How long should men/women be allowed to stay off work after they have children?

> **4** Should everyone be allowed to work from home at least once a week?

> **5** Should employees be allowed to wear to work whatever clothes they want?

5 solutions

LOW TECH SOLUTIONS p56   ASK THE EXPERTS p59   IT'S OUT OF ORDER p62   MAN VERSUS MACHINE p64

SPEAKING	**5.1** Talk about inventions over the last 100 years **5.2** Present and answer questions on your area of expertise **5.3** Explain/Solve problems **5.4** Present a new machine
LISTENING	**5.2** Listen to people answering difficult questions **5.3** Listen to conversations about technical problems **5.4** Watch a BBC programme about a race between a car and two people
READING	**5.1** Read about some low technology solutions **5.2** Read a book review
WRITING	**5.1** Write an advantages/disadvantages essay **5.4** Write an advertisement

BBC INTERVIEWS

Are you good at solving problems?

5.1))) LOW TECH SOLUTIONS

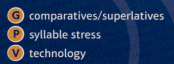

G comparatives/superlatives
P syllable stress
V technology

READING

1 Work in pairs. Discuss the questions.

1 In general, do you like or dislike new technology and gadgets like ebooks, tablets and phones?

2 Can you think of ways in which technology has made our lives better/worse?

3 Are there any problems which technology has helped to solve? Give examples.

2 A Look at the prompts below. What information do you think could go in the gaps to describe the problems? Use the pictures to help you.

1 New _____ tends to make things faster and more efficient.

2 Popular entertainment (theatre, cinema, music concerts, exhibitions) is often _____ and based in cities.

3 In many villages in Asia and Africa, access to _____ is still a huge problem.

4 The citizens of Bogotá, Colombia wanted young people to have more access to _____.

B Read the text to check your answers.

3 A Work in pairs. Answer the questions.

1 How is the Rural Academy (slow theatre) different from other theatre companies?

2 Why might people living in rural areas appreciate this type of theatre?

3 How does the Playpump help children to solve the problem of access to water?

4 How has the pump changed the lives of the young girls in particular?

5 How has the invention of the ebook changed how people read?

6 Where have they put the new libraries in Bogotá?

B Discuss. What do you think of the solutions suggested? Which idea do you like best? Can you think of some other solutions to these problems?

Why is it that people seem to think that the newest technology is always the best? From high-speed trains to high-speed internet, you could be forgiven for thinking that faster is always better (not to mention, more efficient and more economical). We decided to investigate a few simpler, more low-tech solutions to the world's problems.

Meet the slow theatre

Much of our popular entertainment these days is action-packed, expensive and based in cities. So, the Rural Academy decided they wanted to offer an alternative. Touring the United States, they take a horse-drawn theatre, and a bicycle-powered silent cinema on the road with them. They want to celebrate and call attention to life in more rural locations, in opposition to what they see as the global urbanisation of our culture, economy, media and art. By using a carriage pulled by horses, rather than a vehicle that runs on petrol, they offer a less expensive, low-tech alternative entertainment, which they hope will include more people and move at a slightly slower pace.

The roundabout water pump

Access to a clean water supply is still one of the biggest problems for people living in rural villages in Asia and Africa. To try and solve the problem, a company in South Africa has invented a way to use children's high energy levels to help pump water from underground. The Playpump is a water pump that is powered when the children use the roundabout. As they play, the water is pumped from below the ground into a storage tank. Before the pumps were installed, many young girls had to spend hours of their day walking to collect water, rather than going to school. With the new pumps, however, the girls don't need to miss school, so they get a much better education.

Bus stop libraries in Bogotá

The invention of the ebook has meant that books are now slightly cheaper and a lot lighter to carry. But in Bogotá, Colombia, they had a far better idea for helping people to read on the go. The city wanted to improve the access that young people had to books, but not by buying new tablets. They decided to install colourful book libraries around the city, in the parks and at bus stops. What could be better than to sit in the sunshine and read a book while waiting for your bus?

GRAMMAR

COMPARATIVES AND SUPERLATIVES

4 A Read the article again. Underline examples of comparatives and superlatives.

B Look at your examples and complete the rules. How do we form the comparatives and superlatives of common adjectives?

> **RULES**
> **1** Adjectives with one syllable
> comparatives: add _____
> superlatives: add _____
> **2** Adjectives with two or more syllables
> comparatives: add _____
> superlatives: add _____

C Look at the sentences below and complete the rules with *small* or *big*.

a) Entertainment has become a lot/much/far more expensive.

b) Technology has made books a little/a little bit/ slightly cheaper.

> **RULES**
> **1** Use quantifiers *a lot/much/far* to talk about _____ differences.
> **2** Use quantifiers *a little/a little bit/slightly* to talk about _____ differences.

▷ page 76 **LANGUAGE**BANK

5 Complete the statements with the prompts in brackets.

1 The invention of the bicycle made it _____ (lot/easy) for people to travel from one village to another, to meet new people.

2 The world has become a _____ (much/safe) place to live since the invention of antibiotics. People are _____ (far/healthy) now than 100 years ago.

3 The invention of the washing machine has meant that it is _____ (lot/quick) for people to wash their clothes. I think it's _____ (good) invention of the last century.

4 Although we have computers, paper is still _____ (cheap) and _____ (flexible) way to record the written word.

5 Electricity is _____ (important) invention because without it many of the other things we have would not have been possible.

6 The invention of the telephone and the computer have meant that we are _____ (much/busy) now than we were in the past.

VOCABULARY

TECHNOLOGY

6 A Work in pairs. Put the words/phrases in the box into the correct word web.

> ~~electricity~~   nuclear power   antibiotics
> vaccinations   computer networks   motorbikes
> genetic engineering   washing machine
> vacuum cleaner   space travel   commercial aeroplanes
> solar power   communications satellites

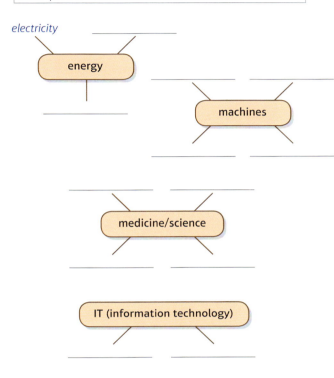

electricity _____

energy

_____

machines

_____

medicine/science

_____

IT (information technology)

_____

B Work in pairs. Can you add any more words to each word web?

C SYLLABLE STRESS Look at the words/phrases above and underline the main stress(es). Sometimes there can be more than one per word/phrase.

electricity   nuclear power

D ▶ 5.1 Listen and check. Then listen again and repeat.

▷ page 82 **VOCABULARY**BANK

SPEAKING

7 A Work in pairs. Choose an invention from the last 100 years. Write two or three sentences to describe how this invention has changed our lives. Don't say what the invention is.

This invention made it much easier to travel from one place to another. Even people in poor societies can use this invention because it does not need petrol.

B Read your sentences to other students. Can they guess the invention?

C Discuss which invention you think has been the best/worst? Why?

WRITING

AN ADVANTAGES/DISADVANTAGES ESSAY; LEARN TO USE DISCOURSE MARKERS

8 A What do you think are the main advantages and disadvantages of technology in everyday life? Write a list.

B Read the model essay. Does it mention any of your ideas?

The advantages and disadvantages of modern technology

1 It is easy to see the advantages of modern technology in our everyday lives. Technology has given us mobile phones, computers, televisions and many other useful things. <u>However</u>, most modern inventions come with a price – maybe social or environmental – so we need to look at both sides of the story.

2 <u>One of the main advantages</u> of modern technology can be seen in medical science. The discoveries of antibiotics and vaccinations have saved millions of lives around the world. <u>In addition</u> to this, modern technology has made industry more efficient.

3 On the other hand, modern technology is responsible for the development of weapons, which have caused a lot of destruction. <u>Another disadvantage</u> is that it makes us lazy. Nowadays, many people spend their lives sitting in front of computer screens. This is a development that surely has negative effects on our mental and physical health, making us more isolated and less active.

4 <u>In my opinion</u>, modern technology is a good thing. In general, the advantages outweigh the disadvantages. Of course there are drawbacks, but it is important to remember that technology itself is not the problem. <u>The problem is that</u> we use technology without always thinking about the harmful consequences.

C Match paragraphs 1–4 with descriptions a)–d).

a) discussion of disadvantages   _____

b) conclusion   _____

c) introduction   _1_

d) discussion of advantages   _____

D Work in pairs. Complete the guidelines for writing an essay with the expressions in the box.

personal opinions   examples   notes   beginning   logical order

1 Sort out the facts – make _____ of all the relevant information you have on the subject.

2 Plan your argument – organise your notes and arrange the ideas in a _____.

3 Give your essay an appropriate _____. Describe what you are planning to say.

4 Decide how many paragraphs you need for your argument. Each paragraph should discuss one point. Use _____ to support your arguments.

5 Write a logical conclusion. Though the style of the essay is generally formal and impersonal, this might be the place to include some _____.

9 A Look at the underlined words and phrases in the essay. Put them in the correct place in the table.

introduce advantages
The most important advantage is …

introduce disadvantages
The main disadvantage is …

contrasting ideas
Although, …

additional reasons
As well as that, …
And another thing, …

personal opinion/conclusion
In general, …
As far as I'm concerned, …

B Underline the correct alternatives.

> **Satellite TV: good or bad?**
> More and more people are watching satellite television. [1]*The main advantage / As well as that* is that you can choose exactly what you want to watch, and [2]*in addition to this / however* you can watch programmes in other languages. [3]*However, / Although* this means that whereas people used to talk about programmes with colleagues and friends, now they usually don't watch the same programmes. [4]*On the other hand / And another thing*, there is too much choice. There are so many programmes to choose from that people can't decide what to watch. [5]*This means that / As far as I'm concerned*, they watch too much television. [6]*In my opinion / The problem is that*, satellite television is a good thing, as it gives people more choice. [7]*However, / In general*, people need to be careful that they choose their programmes carefully.

10 Choose one of the topics below and write an essay about the advantages and disadvantages of it. Look back at Exercises 8 and 9 to help you.

- modern technology in everyday life
- owning a car/bicycle
- playing computer games
- using a digital camera
- using email/text messages
- cheap flights

ASK THE EXPERTS

G question tags
P intonation: question tags
V information; word building: adjectives

5.2

A

B

C

D

F

E

SPEAKING

1 A Match photos A–F to the questions below.

1 Is it possible to surf a tidal wave?
2 Why is snow cold?
3 Is there an easy way to prove the Earth is round?
4 Why do onions make you cry?
5 Is a rainbow hot or cold?
6 Why are sumo wrestlers so fat?

B Work in pairs. How many questions above can you answer in two minutes?

C Turn to page 86 and check your answers.

VOCABULARY

INFORMATION

2 A Match the pairs of verbs in the box with situations 1–5.

question/wonder   discuss/debate   respond/reply
research/investigate   inquire/look into   argue/quarrel

1 Someone tells you something. You are not sure you agree.
question/wonder
2 Someone writes you a letter.
3 There is an interesting topic in class.
4 You disagree with someone and talk angrily with them.
5 You are writing a thesis for your Master's degree.
6 You need to find some information, e.g. about cinema times or to book a table.

B Read the sentences below. In which sentence is *wonder* a verb? In which sentence is it a noun?

a) I wonder if anyone has ever tried to surf a tidal wave.

b) I can name the seven wonders of the world.

C Underline the correct alternative to complete the sentences. Is the correct answer a noun or a verb?

1 The police officer continued his *investigation/wonder/inquire* into the robbery.
2 Didn't you get my email? You didn't *response/look into/reply*.
3 We had a very interesting *discuss/debate/wonder* about the death penalty.
4 I've nearly finished my *research/investigate/reply* into nuclear particles.
5 When I hear about all these social problems, I have to *inquire/question/respond* the education system.
6 You want a job here? No problem. My cousin is the boss. I'll *inquiry/debate/look into* it for you.
7 It was a silly *respond/quarrel/argue*. Now they are friends again.

LISTENING

3 A Work in groups and discuss.

1 How do you prefer to find information, on the internet, in books or by asking people? What does it depend on?
2 What type of questions do children ask? Think of some examples.

They sometimes ask difficult questions like: 'Why is snow cold?'

B Read a review of a book about questions children ask their parents. How did the author get the idea for the book? Are any of your questions included in the examples from the book?

Questions Daddy can't answer

It all began with a question asked by Dean, a four-year-old boy: 'Why do ships have round windows?' His father didn't know. And when his sister started behaving badly, Dean asked another question: 'Why can't we just cook her?' On a long drive the boy wondered why the road was so loud. His father replied, 'Because the people who live next to the road have their vacuum cleaners on.' The boy's inquiries kept coming: 'Why is the sky blue? Are rainbows hot or cold? What was it like living in the 1940s? What would hurt more – getting run over by a car or getting stung by a jellyfish? Why do police officers like doughnuts?'

Eventually, Jamieson decided to write down the questions. He thought it might be fun one day to show them to his son. Then he had a better idea: he'd research the answers. Some people might do their investigations on the internet. Not Mr Jamieson. He contacted experts ranging from astronomers to Buddhist monks, to scientists, to magicians, and asked lots of questions. He later turned these – and the experts' responses – into a book: *Father Knows Less.*

4 A Read five questions from the book *Father Knows Less*. Try to answer them. Compare your ideas with other students.

> How many hairs are there on the human head?
> Why are the windows on ships always round?
> Why is there war?
> Why did The Beatles break up?
> What happens when your plane flies over a volcano?

B ▶ **5.2** Listen to some people trying to answer the questions in Exercise 4A. Are their answers the same as your ideas?

C Listen again and complete the notes.

1 Ships' round windows: _____
2 Number of hairs on a human head: _____
3 A plane flies over a volcano: _____
4 The Beatles broke up: _____
5 Reasons for war: different ideologies, a sense of honour, _____

GRAMMAR
QUESTION TAGS

5 A Complete questions 1–6. Then look at audio script 5.2 on page 91 to check.

1 Round windows are stronger, _____ they?
2 No, it's not that many, _____ it?
3 It depends whose head, _____ it?
4 Nothing happens, _____ it?
5 They got old, _____ they?
6 John Lennon went off with Yoko Ono, _____ he?

B Read the rules about question tags. Which rules are exemplified in 1–6 in Exercise 6A?

Rule 2 is shown in question number 3. It uses doesn't.

> **RULES**
>
> **1** Use question tags to confirm information.
> **2** To form a question tag, repeat the auxiliary verb. For example, use *do* or *does* for the present. Use *will* or *won't* for the future.
> **3** After the auxiliary verb, use a pronoun (e.g. *he, she, it, they*).
> **4** If the sentence is positive, the question tag is negative.
> **5** If the sentence is negative, the question tag is positive.

▷ page 76 **LANGUAGE**BANK

6 Look at the statements below and complete the question tags.

1 You're Italian, *aren't* you?
2 You aren't a doctor, *are* you?
3 You don't smoke, _____ you?
4 You play a musical instrument, _____ you?
5 You didn't know any of the other students before, _____ you?
6 Our teacher hasn't taught you before, _____ she?
7 You will be here tomorrow, _____ you?
8 You went to bed late last night, _____ you?
9 You've travelled a lot, _____ you?
10 You were good at sport when you were a child, _____ you?

7 A ▶ **5.3** **INTONATION: question tags** Listen to two questions. Notice how the intonation goes down when the speaker is sure of the answer. Notice how the intonation goes up when the speaker is not sure.

1 You're Italian, aren't you? (the speaker knows the answer)

2 You aren't a doctor, are you? (the speaker is not sure of the answer)

B ▶ **5.4** Listen to the questions in Exercise 6. Which answers is the speaker sure about? Listen and repeat the questions, using the same intonation.

C Work in pairs. Choose six questions to ask your partner. Make sure your intonation is correct in the question tags.

A: *You play a guitar, don't you?*
B: *Yes, I do. I play bass in a band.*

SPEAKING

8 Work in groups and follow instructions 1–4 below.

1 Think of one subject each that you know a lot about. Write your topics on a piece of paper.
tennis, Japanese cars, hip hop

2 Exchange papers with another group.

3 Think of statements about the subjects. Use question tags.
Rafael Nadal is the best tennis player in history, isn't he? The most popular Japanese car is the Toyota, isn't it?

4 Read your statements to the first group. Are they correct?

VOCABULARY *PLUS*

WORD BUILDING: ADJECTIVES

9 A Read the text below. How was the ice cream cone invented?

> For over a hundred years ice cream was sold mainly in dishes. Then one day, a creative ice cream seller turned a hopeless situation into a profitable one. In 1904, at a festival, he ran out of spoons and dishes. He bought some wafers from a vendor next to him and put the ice cream into them. The customers loved them and the idea spread quickly. The world has been thankful ever since!

B Underline four adjectives in the text and add them to the word web below. Can you think of other examples of adjectives that fit these patterns?

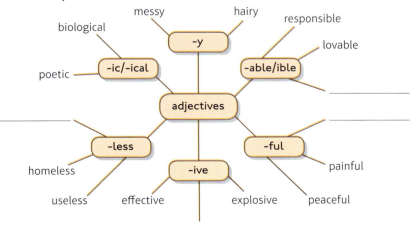

messy   hairy
biological   responsible
                                    lovable
poetic   -y   -able/ible
    -ic/-ical
            adjectives
    -less   -ful
homeless   -ive   painful
useless   effective   explosive   peaceful

speak*out* TIP

Use L1. L1 is your First Language. Some suffixes in your L1 might have similar meanings to suffixes in English. For example, the Italian *-ivo/a* means the same as the English *-ive*. Can you think of any examples from your language?

10 Complete the text. Add suffixes to the words in brackets.

> The city of Detroit, USA was famous for its [1]_____ (value) car industry. In the early days, the city was [2]_____ (response) for the majority of cars in the USA, and Detroit's streets were full of cars. A police officer called William Potts saw that the organisation of the traffic was [3]_____ (hope) and the traffic was very slow. So, in 1920, he developed an [4]_____ (effect) system of lights to regulate the flow of cars. He used the same colours as the railway system and put the lights in a tower so that it would be [5]_____ (ease) for drivers to see them even on [6]_____ (rain) days. Potts's system was very [7]_____ (success). When other countries realised how [8]_____ (use) it was, the system spread all over the world.

11 A Complete the words by adding suffixes.

Find someone who:

1 has a peace*ful*____ hobby.
2 is hope_____ at maths.
3 is a good, care_____ driver.
4 is quite mess_____ at home.
5 thinks he/she is quite creat_____.
6 is quite knowledge_____ about politics.

B Work in groups. Ask and answer questions about the information above.

You've got a peaceful hobby, haven't you?

▷ page 82 **VOCABULARY**BANK

5.3)) IT'S OUT OF ORDER

F polite requests
P intonation: polite requests
V problems and solutions

VOCABULARY

PROBLEMS AND SOLUTIONS

1 A Think of two pieces of technology you have used in the last twenty-four hours. Did you have any problems with them? What problems can you have with them?

B Work in pairs. Look at the photos. What is the problem in each case?

C Look at the phrases in bold. Are they problems (P) or solutions (S)? Which phrases can you use to talk about the problems in pictures A–E above?

1 It's **broken down**.
2 It **needs recharging**.
3 It's **out of order**.
4 It **needs fixing**.
5 There is no **reception** (for my phone).
6 **Try switching it off** (and on again).
7 It **keeps making this strange noise**.
8 It's **crashed/frozen**.
9 It **doesn't work** (any more).
10 We have to **sort it out**.
11 **Save it onto a memory stick**.
12 Shall I **print it for you**?

D Work in pairs and answer the questions.

1 Have any of these problems happened to you or anyone you know recently?
2 How did you feel when it happened?
3 How did you try to solve the problem?

FUNCTION

POLITE REQUESTS

2 A ▶ 5.5 Listen to four conversations. What is the problem in each case?

B Read questions 1–8. Which can you answer? Listen again to check.

1 In conversation 1, what question does the man ask?
2 Where does the woman suggest that he goes?
3 In conversation 2, what does the woman 'keep losing'?
4 What does the man suggest?
5 In conversation 3, what does the vacuum cleaner 'keep making'?
6 Does the woman give the man instructions about what to do to fix his vacuum cleaner?
7 In conversation 4, what does the man ask for?
8 Who does the man need to speak to?

C Complete the extracts in the table with the correct words.

Could you	[1] _____ the line, please? [2] _____ me a refund?
Could you tell me	who I should [3] _____ to? what the [4] _____ is?
Do you know	what the problem is? if there's another [5] _____ somewhere?
Would you mind	[6] _____ at it for me? [7] _____ him for me?

C ▶ 5.6 Listen and repeat the requests.

▷ page 76 **LANGUAGE**BANK

LEARN TO

RESPOND TO REQUESTS

3 A Read some conversation extracts from Exercise 2. Complete the responses with the phrases in the box.

> Yes, I can   I'm not sure   I'm afraid I can't
> Yes, of course (x2)   Of course not   Sure/OK
> Let me have a look

1 M: Do you know if there's another machine somewhere? I really need to get some money.
W: Hmm … _____. There might be one in the shopping centre.

2 W: Would you mind looking at it for me?
M: _____.

3 W: Do you know what the problem is?
M: _____.

4 W: Could you tell me what the problem is, sir?
M: _____. It keeps making a funny noise. And it's just not working properly.

5 W: Could you hold the line, please?
M: _____.

6 M: Could you give me a refund?
W: _____ do that.
M: Well, could you tell me who I should speak to?
W: _____. You need to speak to the manager.
M: OK. Would you mind calling him for me?
W: _____. I'll just call him.

B Read audio script 5.5 on page 91 to check.

4 A Make polite requests and responses with the prompts in brackets.

1 A: I can't concentrate. (Would / mind / turn / music down)?
B: Sure. Sorry about that.

2 A: I need to speak to the manager. (Do / know / if / anyone in the office)?
B: Let me have a look.

3 A: I'm afraid Mr Soul isn't here at the moment.
B: (Do / know / when / coming back)?
A: (not / sure). Do you want me to check?
B: Thank you.

4 A: (Could / tell / how / machine works)? I don't know how to turn it on.
B: (Yes / course).

5 A: I need to take this machine to the repair service. (Would / mind / help / me)?
B: (course / not). Leave it here.

6 A: My computer has frozen. (Could / tell / who / I / speak / to)?
B: OK. (Let / have / look).

B ▶ **5.7** Listen to check your answers.

C INTONATION: polite requests Does the speaker's voice start high or low? Listen again and repeat the requests copying the polite intonation.

SPEAKING

5 A Work in pairs. Read your role and think about the phrases you are going to use. Then role-play the situation below.

Student B

> You need to call your sister but you can't get any reception on your phone. Ask Student A if he/she knows where you can get reception.

Student A

> Tell Student B that you have reception on your phone.
> Suggest that he/she tries standing outside.

> You still can't get any reception. Ask Student A if you can borrow his/her phone to send a text message.

> Tell Student B he/she can borrow your phone to make the phone call.

> Thank Student A for his/her help.

B Change roles and role-play the situation below.

Student A

> You can't get the printer to work. Ask Student B if he/she can help you.

Student B

> Suggest Student A tries turning it off and then on again. Ask if that has worked.

> It still doesn't work. Ask Student B if he/she knows of other printers in the building.

> Tell Student A he/she can use your printer.

> Thank Student B for his/her help.

C Choose one or two situations from Exercises 4 and 5. Write a conversation using the flow charts above to help. Then role-play it with a partner.

DVD PREVIEW

1 Work in pairs and answer the questions.

1 Look at the person on page 65. What type of sport is he doing?

2 Would you like to try this sport? Why?/Why not?

2 Read about the programme. Who do you think will win the race? Why?

Top Gear

BBC

Top Gear is the BBC's international award-winning television series about motor vehicles, mainly cars. More than 350 million viewers worldwide enjoy watching the presenters with their quirky, humorous style. On the show they compare and test-drive cars, and organise all kinds of crazy races. In this programme, James May, possibly the slowest driver in Great Britain, challenges two freerunners to a race in Liverpool city centre. James has to drive six miles towards the Liver building in the city centre in a Peugeot 207. The two teenagers who try to beat him will run and jump over buildings, taking a much more direct route. Who do you think will get there first?

3 Watch the DVD to see if you were right. Number the events in the correct order.

a) The men jump over James's car. _____

b) James arrives at the Liver building. _____

c) James checks his speed. _____

d) The men jump over people eating at a restaurant. _____

e) James stops at a red traffic light. _____

4 Watch the DVD again. What does James May say? Complete the phrases.

1 As we can see, it's a very pretty car, but is it any _____?

2 I'm going to have a race, and it's against the latest French development in urban transport solutions: a couple of young men in silly _____.

3 Parkour: that's a French invention, and involves that sort of thing. Running around the _____ leaping across buildings and benches.

4 Come on – we're not all _____!

5 I must have averaged ten or twelve miles an hour. I should _____.

6 They are not here. No sign of combat trousers man. I've _____!

speakout present a new machine

5 A Work in pairs. Answer the questions and complete the tasks.

1 Write a list of things you have to do every day.

2 Are there any things on this list which you don't enjoy? Could a machine do them for you?

3 Invent a machine which would help you do one of the things. Draw a picture of your machine.

B ▶ 5.8 Listen to someone talking about a new machine. What is the invention? What does it do?

C Listen again and tick the key phrases he uses.

> **KEYPHRASES**
>
> I'm going to tell you about …
> Basically, …
> The way it works is this.
> It works like this …
> First of all, ….
> Then/Also, you can …
> All you have to do is …
> Make sure you …
> The best thing about it is that …

D Prepare and practise a short presentation about your new machine. Use your picture and the useful phrases to explain how it works.

E Present your ideas to the class. Which invention do you think is the best?

writeback an advertisement

6 A Read the advertisement and answer the questions. What is the musical shower? How does it work?

The musical shower

If you like listening to music when you have a shower, then you might already have a stereo in your bathroom. But imagine how much better it would be if your shower-head also had an MP3 player attached to it.

It will download your favourite tunes, or radio programmes at night. Then in the morning, your shower will automatically play your favourite tunes for you. Try our musical shower. There's no better way to start the day.

B Write an advertisement (advert) for your invention (120–180 words). Use the advert above and the key phrases to help.

Ⓖ COMPARATIVES/ SUPERLATIVES

1 A Look at the information and complete sentences (1–4) using the prompts in brackets.

100 years ago in the US: the average life expectancy was forty-seven years, only eight percent of homes had a phone, the maximum speed limit in most cities was ten miles per hour, the average wage was twenty-two cents per hour, and ninety percent of all doctors had no college education.

1 100 years ago, people didn't live _____ as they do today. (long)

2 It used to be _____ to communicate with people on the other side of the world. (far, difficult)

3 It is _____ for modern businesses to pay their employees. (far, expensive)

4 Nowadays, doctors are _____ than they were in the past. (much, educated)

B Write sentences about a hundred years ago. Compare them with your partner.

Ⓥ TECHNOLOGY

2 A Complete the words in sentences 1–6.

1 I don't agree with nu_____ po_____. I think it's a dangerous way of making el_____.

2 Sp_____ tr_____ is a waste of money. Why do we need to send people to the Moon?

3 I couldn't live without my wa_____ ma_____. I hate dirty clothes.

4 I had to have loads of va_____ when I went to Malawi. I didn't want to get ill.

5 I think ge_____ en_____ is a bit worrying. People might start to only want babies which are beautiful.

6 Doctors give people too many an_____. So now, some medicines don't work any more.

B Work in pairs. Choose three sentences you disagree with. Tell your partner why.

Ⓖ INFORMATION

3 A Put the letters in italics in the correct order to find words related to questions.

1 In class last week, we *used discs* …
In class last week, we discussed …

2 I can't answer *nose quits* about …

3 I try to *pen rods* quickly to …

4 In the next few months I'm going to *took lion* … (2 words)

5 I recently *quid rein* about …

6 I *own red* what happened to …

7 I enjoy a good *tea bed* especially about …

8 It would be interesting to *sit negative* a crime like …

B Complete the sentences so that they are true for you.

Ⓖ QUESTION TAGS

4 A Complete the sentences with the correct question tag.

1 She wrote the first *Harry Potter* book in a café, <u>didn't she</u>?

2 This man, who is U2's singer, does a lot of humanitarian work, _____?

3 This actor has won an Oscar for *Forrest Gump*, _____?

4 He was probably the greatest basketball player in history, _____?

5 She lived in Calcutta, where she helped street children, but she wasn't from India, _____?

6 He became Cuba's leader in 1959 and he didn't transfer power to his brother until 2006, _____?

7 Her full name is Madonna Louise Ciccone, _____?

8 Her husband was US President. She's very popular but she probably won't be as famous as him, _____?

B Who are these sentences about?

1 J K Rowling

C Work in groups. One student thinks of a famous person. The others ask tag questions to find out who it is.

A: *You're a man, aren't you?*
B: *Yes.*

Ⓕ POLITE REQUESTS

5 A Match requests 1–5 with responses a)–e).

1 Excuse me, could you tell me where I can find the bathroom?

2 Could you call me a taxi?

3 Would you mind helping me with my bags? They're very heavy.

4 Would you mind opening the window?

5 Could you tell me what time the restaurant opens?

a) Sure. It's very hot in here, isn't it?

b) Yes, of course. It's just over there, down the stairs and on the left.

c) Yes, of course. Where do you want to go to?

d) I'm not sure. Let me have a look. Yes, it opens at 11a.m.

e) Of course not. Let me take your suitcase.

B Work in pairs. Take turns to practise the conversations using the prompts below.

Student A:
• where/bathroom?
• call/taxi?
• shop/close?
• get/door?

Student B
• open/window?
• restaurant/open?
• help/shopping?
• tell/platform the train leaves from?

IRREGULAR VERBS

Verb	Past simple	Past participle
be	was	been
beat	beat	beaten
become	became	become
begin	began	begun
bend	bent	bent
bet	bet	bet
bite	bit	bitten
bleed	bled	bled
blow	blew	blown
break	broke	broken
bring	brought	brought
broadcast	broadcast	broadcast
build	built	built
burn	burned/burnt	burned/burnt
burst	burst	burst
buy	bought	bought
catch	caught	caught
choose	chose	chosen
come	came	come
cost	cost	cost
cut	cut	cut
deal	dealt	dealt
dig	dig	dug
do	did	done
draw	drew	drawn
dream	dreamed/dreamt	dreamed/dreamt
drink	drank	drunk
drive	drove	driven
eat	ate	eaten
fall	fell	fallen
feel	felt	felt
feed	fed	fed
fight	fought	fought
find	found	found
fly	flew	flown
forbid	forbade	forbidden
forget	forgot	forgotten
forgive	forgave	forgiven
freeze	froze	frozen
get	got	got
give	gave	given
go	went	gone
grow	grew	grown
hang	hung	hung
have	had	had
hear	heard	heard
hide	hid	hidden
hit	hit	hit
hold	held	held
hurt	hurt	hurt
keep	kept	kept
know	knew	known
lay	laid	laid
lead	led	led
leap	leapt	leapt
learn	learned/learnt	learned/learnt

Verb	Past simple	Past participle
leave	left	left
lend	lent	lent
let	let	let
lie	lay	lain
light	lit	lit
lose	lost	lost
make	made	made
mean	meant	meant
meet	met	met
mistake	mistook	mistaken
pay	paid	paid
put	put	put
read /riːd/	read /red/	read /red/
ride	rode	ridden
ring	rang	rung
rise	rose	risen
run	ran	run
say	said	said
see	saw	seen
sell	sold	sold
send	sent	sent
set	set	set
shake	shook	shaken
shine	shone	shone
shoot	shot	shot
show	showed	shown
shrink	shrank	shrunk
shut	shut	shut
sing	sang	sung
sink	sank	sunk
sit	sat	sat
sleep	slept	slept
slide	slid	slid
smell	smelled/smelt	smelled/smelt
speak	spoke	spoken
spell	spelt	spelt
spend	spent	spent
spill	spilled/spilt	spilled/spilt
split	split	split
spread	spread	spread
stand	stood	stood
steal	stole	stolen
stick	stuck	stuck
sting	stung	stung
swim	swam	swum
take	took	taken
teach	taught	taught
tear	tore	torn
tell	told	told
think	thought	thought
throw	threw	thrown
understand	understood	understood
wake	woke	woken
wear	wore	worn
win	won	won
write	wrote	written

GRAMMAR

1.1 question forms

object questions

Object questions use the word order: question word + auxiliary verb + subject + infinitive.

question word	auxiliary verb	subject	verb
Where	do	you	work?
What	did	she	say?
When	are	they	coming?

yes/no questions

Yes/No questions don't use a question word. The answer to the question is *Yes* or *No*.

auxiliary verb	subject	verb
Does	he	smoke?
Did	we	win?
Have	they	arrived?

subject questions

When the *wh-* question word is the subject of the question:
- we don't use an auxiliary verb (*do, did*, etc.).
- we use the same word order as in an affirmative sentence.

question word	verb	object
Who	wants	ice cream?
What	happened?	
Who	ate	the cheese?

questions with prepositions

When we use a verb + preposition expression (but not multi-word verbs) such as *look for, depend on, write about,* etc., we usually keep the verb and preposition together:
*What did you **talk about**?   Who are you **looking for**?*

In very formal English we sometimes move the preposition to the front of the sentence. Compare:
*What does it **depend on**?   On what does it **depend**?*

1.2 review of verb tenses

present simple

+	He **looks** happy.
–	He **doesn't look** happy.
?	**Does** he **look** happy?

Use the present simple to talk about something that is always or generally true, habits, routines, with *be* and other state verbs (see below).

present continuous

+	We're **staying** here.
–	We **aren't staying** here.
?	**Are** we **staying** here?

Use the present continuous to talk about an activity happening at the time of speaking or a temporary activity happening around now. It may be happening at the moment, but maybe not.

past simple

+	They **worked** hard.
–	They **didn't work** hard.
?	**Did** they **work** hard?

Use the past simple to talk about finished actions, events or situations in the past.

past continuous

+	I **was living** there during the 90s.
–	I **wasn't living** there during the 90s.
?	**Were** you **living** there?

Use the past continuous to talk about an action or situation in progress at a particular time in the past. This action was not finished at that time.

state verbs and dynamic verbs

State verbs are not usually used in the continuous form. The most common state verbs are:
- attitude verbs: *love, hate, like, want, prefer*
- thinking verbs: *believe, know, remember, understand, mean, imagine*
- sense verbs: *see, hear, sound, appear, seem*
- belonging verbs: *own, possess, belong to, have, contain, include*

Some state verbs can be used in the continuous form when they describe actions, e.g. *see, have, think*:
*I'm **seeing** Phil tonight.* (see = meet)
*We're **having** a party.* (have = organise)
*I'm **thinking** of going to university.* (think = consider)

1.3 talking about yourself

introducing a question
Could I ask a question?
There are a couple of things I'd like to ask about.
Can I ask you about that?
I have a query.

introducing an opinion
For me (the most important thing is) …
I'd have to say …
In my opinion, …
One thing I'd like to say is that …

PRACTICE

1.1

A Write questions for the answers in italics.

1 Where _____ ?
   I live *in Madrid*.
2 Who _____ ?
   Nick won the game.
3 Does _____ ?
   No, he doesn't eat meat.
4 What _____ ?
   They are *sleeping*.
5 What _____ ?
   I'm writing about *my first holiday*.
6 When _____ ?
   We arrived *yesterday*.
7 Who _____ ?
   We ate the chocolate.
8 Did _____ ?
   Yes, we liked the film.

B Put the words in brackets in the correct places to make questions.

1 the President? (killed, who)
   _____
2 were you thinking? (what, about)
   _____
3 to the old theatre? (happened, what)
   _____
4 Where your great-grandparents come? (from, did)
   _____
5 your ancestors from here? (come, did)
   _____
6 she here for a long time? (worked, has)
   _____
7 is all that noise? (who, making)
   _____
8 house you looking for? (are, which)
   _____

1.2

A Underline the correct alternatives.

'Like most translators, I ¹*'m speaking/speak* several languages. At the moment, I ²*'m attending/attend* a conference. I ³*was doing/did* some work for an internet company when I ⁴*was hearing/heard* about this conference. I ⁵*was arriving/arrived* three days ago and I'm going to stay until Monday, when it ends.'

My best friend is called Gina. We ⁶*aren't speaking/don't speak* to each other every day, but we're very close. I ⁷*was meeting/met* her on my first morning at university. I ⁸*was looking/looked* for the library when she came up to me and asked, 'Excuse me, ⁹*do you know/ are you knowing* where the library is?' We ¹⁰*were finding/ found* it together!

B Put the verbs in brackets into the correct tense.

1 Sit down and watch the game! We _____ (win) 2–1. Ronaldo scored two minutes ago.
2 John wasn't here last summer. He _____ (travel) around Africa.
3 Fifty years ago, my favourite writer _____ (die).
4 I didn't do the homework because I _____ (not listen) when the teacher told us what to do.
5 DVDs _____ (not work) very well on my laptop, so I use the TV and DVD player.
6 What's that smell? Can you turn off the oven? I think the food _____ (burn).
7 _____ (see) that film last night? What did you think?
8 Everyone knows that smoking _____ (cause) cancer.

1.3

A Find and correct the mistakes in the conversation below. There are six mistakes.

A: There are a couple of things I'd like ask about.
B: Go ahead.
A: Firstly, which of your films do you think is the best?
B: I'd having to say *Millennium Dreamer*. For me, it's my best film and it was my first comedy.
A: Can I ask you around that? You've never done comedy before. Why not?
B: I don't know. I suppose people think I'm a serious actor.
A: Could I ask question about your image? Is it accurate? Are you really the strong silent type in real life?
B: No. One of thing I'd like to say is that these images are invented by the media. By my opinion, good actors are never just one thing. That's why they're actors.

GRAMMAR

2.1 present perfect and past simple

Present perfect simple: *have/has* + past participle (*lived, worked, seen* etc.)

+	I**'ve been** to Poland a few times.
–	He **hasn't worked** here before.
?	**Have** you **bought** a new car?

For irregular past participles see the list of irregular verbs on page 67.

time up to now

Use the present perfect for actions which have happened in your life before now. These are often general experiences. It isn't important exactly when these things happened. Conversations which begin like this in the present perfect usually continue in the past simple as the speaker adds details:

I've been to Colombia. Really? Where did you go?
He's played in an Indie band. What were they called?

We often use the adverbs *ever* and *never* with the present perfect:

We've never been to China.   Have you ever been to the Opera?

recent events

Use the present perfect to talk about events which happened a short time ago. We often use the adverbs *just, yet* and *already*:

I've just finished his book. It was brilliant.
We've already eaten.
Have you done your homework yet?
We've seen a lot of Jude recently.

present perfect or past simple?

Use the past simple to talk about a specific event which happened at a specific time:

I've been to Sweden.
(At some time in my life up to now. We don't know when.)
We went to Stockholm in 2002.
NOT ~~We've been to Stockholm in 2002.~~
(This is a specific occasion and date, so we use the past simple.)

2.2 narrative tenses

past simple

Use the past simple for states and actions in the past. We often specify the time when they happened:

I left university in 1996.   He didn't know the way to Sal's house.

past continuous

Use the past continuous to talk about the background information for a story. Use the past simple to talk about the main events.

BACKGROUND INFORMATION		MAIN EVENT
past continuous		past simple
I **was walking** through the park …	WHEN	… I **heard** a noise
The sun **was shining** …		
The birds **were singing** …		
past ~~~~~~~~~~~~~~~~~~~~~~~~~~		now

As I was walking through the park, the sun was shining and the birds were singing. Suddenly, I heard a loud noise.

Often the past continuous action is interrupted by another action (in the past simple):

I was having a bath when the phone rang.

We can use conjunctions like *as* and *while* to talk about two actions which were happening at the same time:

While I was reading the paper, I watched the women buying vegetables in the market.

For more information on state and dynamic verbs section 1.2, page 68.

past perfect

+	I **had finished** my work.
–	They **hadn't had** time.
?	**Had** they **been** there before?

Use the past perfect to make it clear that one action happened before the other.

past perfect	past simple	present
I lost my wallet.	*I didn't have any money.*	
past ——————+————————+————		now

I didn't have any money because I had lost my wallet.

When *before* or *after* is used in the sentence, it's already clear which action comes before the other, so we can use the past simple instead of the past perfect:

She had lived in London for five years before she moved to New York.
She lived in London for five years before she moved to New York.

We often use the past perfect with 'thinking' verbs like *remember, realise, think, discover, find out*, etc.:

When I got to the school, I realised I'd left my books at home.

2.3 telling a story

beginning the story	This happened when … In the beginning, …
describing what happened	Well, … Anyway, … Before long, … So, … And then, all of a sudden … The next thing I knew, …
ending the story	In the end, … Finally, …

questions to keep a story going	So, what happened? What did you do? What happened next? Really?
responses to show interest	I don't believe it! Oh no. / Oh dear. How embarrassing! That's really funny. You must be joking. Yes, I know.

PRACTICE

2.1

A Tick the correct sentences, a) or b).

1 a) I've been to India last year.
  b) I went to India last year.
2 a) I finished my studies in 2005.
  b) I've finished my studies in 2005.
3 a) Did you have lunch yet?
  b) Have you had lunch yet?
4 a) Did you ever see *Metallica* play live?
  b) Have you ever seen *Metallica* play live?
5 a) Is this the first time you've tried judo?
  b) Is this the first time you tried judo?
6 a) It's the most beautiful place I've ever been to.
  b) It's the most beautiful place I ever went to.

B Use the prompts to make short conversations.

1 A: you / be / here / before? (ever)
  B: no / not
2 A: you / see / the film *The Reader*?
  B: no / not / see (yet)
3 A: he / be / to Budapest?
  B: yes / go / last summer
4 A: you / finish / that book? (yet)
  B: yes / start / the next one (already)
5 A: you / see / Maria?
  B: yes, she / leave / a message for you
6 A: he / decide / what job / want to do? (yet)
  B: no / have / not

2.2

A Underline the correct alternatives to complete the story.

I remember when Marvin Gaye [1]*died/had died*. I [2]*had been/was going* to one of his concerts a few months before. In fact, he [3]*hadn't played/wasn't playing* very well and I was disappointed. I also remember when JFK was shot. I [4]*had lived/was living* with my parents in New York and I [5]*studied/was studying* at the time. I remember the cleaning lady [6]*came/was coming* into the room, and said to me, 'Hey, President Lincoln has been shot.' I [7]*replied/was replying*, 'I know that.' 'No,' she said. 'President Lincoln has been shot!' So I said, 'What do you mean?' And she said, 'Oh no, I mean … President, you know, what's his name, the one now. President Kennedy's been shot.' So then I [8]*was turning/turned* on the radio.

B Find and correct the mistakes. One sentence is correct.

1 I was leaving the room when I had heard someone shouting.
2 I couldn't open the door because I left my keys at home.
3 We drove through the tunnel when the car broke down.
4 As soon as the film started I realised I seen it before.
5 I never been to Egypt before, so I was really excited to see the pyramids.
6 By the time we arrived at the party, everybody else is leaving.
7 We had waited for nearly an hour before the waiter took our order.
8 I looked through some old photographs when I found this one of you.

2.3

A Complete the conversation with the words and phrases in the box.

In the end   don't believe it   The next thing I knew   this happened when
So, what happened   Well   really funny   Anyway   You must be joking   So

A: Well, [1]_____ I was working in a photographic store.
B: [2]_____?
A: [3]_____, one day a woman came in and asked if we could fix the problem she had with a photograph. [4]_____ I asked her what the problem was.
B: OK.
A: [5]_____, she had taken this old photo out of her bag which showed an old man sitting behind a cow, milking it. [6]_____, when I asked her what she wanted us to do to the photo, she said, 'Can you move the cow?' 'Move the cow?' I asked. 'Yes,' she replied. 'I want to see what my grandfather looked like.' She pointed to the feet sticking out from under the cow.

B: Oh no. [7]_____.
A: No, seriously. She wanted us to move the cow, so that she could see her grandfather's face.
B: I [8]_____! So, what happened next?
A: [9]_____, when I told her we couldn't do it, she got quite angry, and left the shop saying, 'Then I'll have to take it to someone else.'
B: That's [10]_____.

GRAMMAR

3.1   the future (plans)

be going to

+	I'm going to start university next year.
–	He isn't going to get a job this year.
?	Where are you going to stay?

When using be going to use the word order: subject + *am/are/is* + *going to* + infinitive without to. Use *be going to* to talk about future plans or intentions. When the verb is *go* or *come*, we often use the present continuous:
We're going to (go to) Spain. We're going to Spain.
I'm going to come and see you later. I'm coming to see you later.

present continuous

+	I'm starting my course in September.
–	We're not going away for very long.
?	What time are you leaving in the morning?

The present continuous is formed: subject + *am/are/is* (*not*) + verb + *-ing*. Use the present continuous to talk about future plans, when arrangements have already been made. We usually specify a future time such as *next week*, *on Friday*, etc., unless it is already clear that we are talking about the future:
We're flying to Greece on Friday. (We've already bought the tickets.)
She's staying in a hotel near the airport. (The hotel is already booked.)
In some cases it doesn't matter if it's the present continuous or *be going to*:
I'm playing football on Saturday.
I'm going to play football on Saturday.

will

+	We'll meet you at the station.
–	I won't see you tomorrow.
?	Will you want a taxi?

When there is no plan or arrangement (when we make a decision at the time of speaking), we often use *will*: *I'm tired. I think I'll go to bed.* (subject + *will* + infinitive)
For use of *be going to* and *will* for prediction, see section 3.2 below.

might

+	I might go out later.
–	We might not be able to finish all this work tomorrow.

Use *might* + infinitive without to to talk about plans, when we are unsure what the plan is:
I might stay at home and watch a DVD.
(But I'm not sure. I might go out.)

spoken grammar

We do not usually use *might* + infinitive without to in the question form. It seems old-fashioned and formal:
Do you think you might see Evelyn?
NOT ~~Might you see Evelyn?~~

3.2   the future (predictions)

will
Use *will* to make predictions:
Smartphones will organise our lives.
She's so talented that I'm sure she'll become famous.
We often use *I think* and *I hope* with *will*:
I think John will become a doctor.
She hopes she will work in the theatre.

be going to
Use *be going to* to make predictions when there is present evidence:
We only have two cars. It's going to be difficult to take eleven people tomorrow.
We use *probably* to make the prediction less certain. *Probably* usually comes after *will*:

The dollar will probably get stronger this year.
Probably comes after *to be* when we use it with *be going to*:
E-readers are probably going to become cheaper.

may and *might*
Use *may* or *might* to make predictions which are less certain. The negative forms are *may not* and *might not*:
Some of our workers may lose their jobs because of the restructuring.
We might not go away this year because we don't have any money.

could
Use *could* to make predictions which are less certain:

Global warming could destroy large parts of Asia in the next thirty years.

be likely to
Use *be likely to* to make predictions when something is probable. The negative is *be unlikely to* or *not be likely to*:
Regina is likely to be late because she works until seven.
We're unlikely to reach Paris before lunch because of all the traffic.
Are you likely to be hungry later?
Likely/Unlikely are adjectives:
Will we start at 5.00? It's unlikely.

spoken grammar
Might is more common than may in spoken English.
May is a little bit more formal.

3.3   dealing with misunderstandings

saying you didn't hear something	I didn't catch any of that.
saying you don't understand someone's opinion	You've lost me. I don't get what you're saying.
asking someone to explain something more clearly	What exactly do you mean? Do you mean to say …?
asking someone to repeat something	Can you say that again? Could you repeat the last part/name/thing you said?

PRACTICE

3.1

A Complete the conversation. Use the prompts in brackets where necessary.

A: Where ¹_____ you going?

B: I'm ²_____ to Paul's house. We' ³_____ going to watch the football.

A: OK. Who ⁴_____? (play)

B: Real Madrid versus Barcelona.

A: I see. And what time are you ⁵_____ home? (come)

B: I don't know.

A: How ⁶_____ getting home?

B: I'm not sure. I ⁷_____ his dad to drive me home, or I ⁸_____ catch the bus. (ask/might)

B Find and correct the mistakes. There is one mistake in each sentence.

1 Will you going out this weekend?

2 I'm sorry I can't come. I playing tennis after work.

3 I don't feel very well. I think I stay at home.

4 What you going to do?

5 We go for a picnic, so I hope it doesn't rain.

6 Is that the phone? Don't worry – I'm going to get it.

7 They might going to a concert.

8 I'm sorry we can't come, but we going to visit my mother this weekend.

3.2

A Rewrite the sentences below using the words in brackets.

1 We probably won't win the cup this year. (might)
We _____

2 I may be late. (likely)
I'm _____

3 That company will close in July. (going)
That company _____

4 He probably won't call after 10.00. (unlikely)
He _____

5 I'm not going to give up exercise. (won't)
I _____

6 We might have a problem with the flight. (may)
There _____

7 She'll get angry when she sees this. (going)
She _____

8 Are you going to visit us? (will)
_____

9 I would love it if he comes to the party. (hope)
_____

10 It is thought prices will rise if they complete the development. (could)
Prices _____

B Put the pairs of words in the box into the correct place to complete the sentences.

will be	aren't going	won't know	might not
likely to	may arrive	is going	not likely

1 Jenny be able to meet us tonight because she has to work late.

2 Several of our workers are lose their jobs this year because of the economic recession.

3 In twenty years' time, cars able to fly.

4 The predicted storm at any moment.

5 The children to stay with me because I'm busy.

6 I my exam results until August.

7 It's that we'll arrive before 6.00 because there are train delays.

8 Watch out! That painting to fall off the wall!

3.3

A Match 1–7 with a)–g) to make sentences and questions.

1 I didn't catch   a) you're saying.

2 You've lost   b) you mean?

3 I don't get what   c) that again?

4 What exactly do   d) to say …?

5 Could you repeat the e) any of that.

6 Do you mean   f) last name?

7 Can you say   g) me.

You're where? Don't shush me!

SUSHI BAR

GRAMMAR

4.1 *must, have to, should* (obligation)

must, have to

+	I **must** get up at 5 tomorrow. They **have to** start work early. We **must** start on time. She **has to** get there early.
−	You **mustn't** do that! We **don't have to** worry. They **mustn't** be late. He **doesn't have to** bring anything.
?	Do I/we/you **have to** bring …? (**Must** you go so early?)* **Does** he/she/it **have to** go?

*Question forms with *must* are not very common, and sound quite formal. We usually use *Do I have to …?* instead.

Use *must* and *have to* to talk about obligations. These things are necessary or important. *Must* is often used for a personal obligation (something we have decided for ourselves that we must do):

*I **must** give up eating chocolate.*

Must is also used in written rules:

*All applicants **must** provide proof of identity.*

Have to is used for external obligation:

*We **have to** wear a uniform.* (It's a company rule.)

Often you can use *must* or *have to* with the same meaning, but in spoken English *have to* is more common.

Don't have to and *mustn't* have different meanings.

Mustn't means 'it is not allowed'. *Don't/Doesn't have to* means it is not necessary, but you can do it if you want:

*You **mustn't** smoke cigarettes anywhere in the building.* (It is not permitted and it's dangerous.)

*You **don't have to** work after 6.* (It's not necessary.)

Must can only be used to talk about present or future obligation. To talk about a past obligation, use *had to*:

*We **had to** get up early to catch the plane.*

spoken grammar

Have/Has got to means the same as *have/has to* in the context of obligation and is used a lot in spoken English:

*I**'ve got to** get some money from the bank.*
*She**'s got to** get another job.*

should/shouldn't

+	I/You/He/She/ It/We/They	**should** see this film.
−		**shouldn't** smoke in the house.
?	Do you think we **should** …?*	

*Should we … is more formal, and not very common.

Use *should* to talk about weak obligations (not as strong as *must* or *have to*). Often it is used for things which you think are a good idea (advice):

*You **should** come to work in smart clothes.*

Use *shouldn't* to talk about things which are not a good idea:

*You **shouldn't** go to bed so late.*

Ought to has the same meaning as *should*, but is not usually used in the negative or questions:

*You **ought to** call her. = You should call her.*

4.2 *used to, would*

used to

+	I/You/He/She/ It/We/They	**used to** live in France.
−		**didn't use to** see my parents.
?	Did they **use to** visit?	

Use *used to* to talk about past habits/states, which have often changed or are not true now. You can also use the past simple.

*As a child, I **used to** love eating sweets.*
*As a child I **ate** a lot of sweets.*

We can also use *would* to talk about past habits, but not to talk about past states.

*I **would** go to the sweet shop every day.* (habit)
*As a child, I **was** very happy.*
*As a child I **used to be** very happy.* (state)
NOT *As a child, I would be very happy.* (state)

Do not use *used to* to talk about things that happened only once, or for a specific number of times/length of time. Use the past simple for this:

*My family **moved** to America last year.*
NOT *My family used to move to America last year.*
*We **went** to Italy twice on holiday.*
NOT *We used to go to Italy twice on holiday.*
*I **studied** at university for three years.*
NOT *I used to study at university for three years.*

spoken grammar

Never used to is more common in spoken English than *didn't use to*.

*We **never used to** see them, except for during August.*

In short answers in spoken English, we often leave out the verb or phrase after *used to*.

*Do you smoke? No, I **used to**, but I don't any more.*

4.3 reaching agreement

giving opinions

I (really) feel that …
The way I see things, …
The way I see it, …

suggestions

What about …?
I suggest we focus on …
I think we should think about …
I suggest we think about …
How about if / Why don't we (call it)…?

commenting on other opinions

That's a good idea. That's a good point. That's fine by me. That's OK by me. Exactly!	I (don't) see what you mean. I'm not sure that I agree, actually. I'm not sure that … is a good idea.

PRACTICE

4.1

A Underline the correct alternative to complete the text.

The worst jobs in the world?

If you like travelling to exotic places, perhaps you ¹*should/shouldn't* try this job. Helge Zieler is a mosquito researcher. In order to study the biting habits of the mosquito which spreads malaria in Brazil, Helge ²*has to/doesn't have to* sit inside a mosquito net while hundreds of mosquitoes bite him. Every time he sees a mosquito land on his body, he ³*must/have to* suck it into a tube in his mouth, and then blow it into a container. On a good evening, Helge can catch 500 mosquitoes in three hours. But to do this, he receives 3,000 bites (an average of seventeen bites per minute for 180 minutes). He ⁴*mustn't/must* forget his anti-malaria tablets. Once he caught malaria and it took him two years to recover.

You ⁵*shouldn't/don't have to* drive too fast on the roads, especially when you're driving in the countryside. Why? Because more than 400 million animals are killed on the roads every year. Joanne Keene knows, because she ⁶*has to/shouldn't* remove them. Car drivers ⁷*don't have to/must* pick the animals up, so Joanne drives around in a huge truck full of dead cats and raccoons. 'It's a hard job,' she says, 'because we work very long hours. We ⁸*mustn't/must* be on call 24 hours a day.'

B Match 1–8 with a)–h) to make sentences.

1 It's a good job but we …
2 I love Saturday mornings, because I don't have to
3 I think you should
4 The doctor told me that I
5 You mustn't
6 You don't have to
7 Francois is very lucky. His father is very rich, so he
8 I really must

a) have to work hard.
b) should do more exercise.
c) come to work dressed in jeans. You have to look smart.
d) doesn't have to work at all.
e) give up smoking. It's not good for my health.
f) get up for work. I can stay in bed until 10a.m.
g) send the forms in until September, but it's a good idea to send them early.
h) think about whether you really want to apply for the job.

4.2

A Cross out the alternative which is not possible.

1 I *used to play/played/play* a lot of tennis when I was younger.
2 After school I *would take/used to take/take* the bus home.
3 He *never used to play/would play/played* the guitar, but he doesn't play any more.
4 I *didn't use to enjoy/didn't enjoy/wouldn't enjoy* school, but I worked hard anyway.
5 Tim *used to have/would have/had* long hair.
6 I *studied/used to study/didn't use to study* French for five years.

B Make sentences with used to or would using the words in brackets. Sometimes both may be possible.

1 In Ancient Greece, people _____ (think) the world was flat, but Aristotle thought it was round.
2 In the olden days, people _____ (not have) cars, so they rode horses.
3 _____ people really _____ (enjoy) watching gladiator fights in Ancient Rome?
4 In the sixteenth century, ladies _____ (put) a white powder containing lead on their faces. It was poisonous.
5 Two hundred years ago, they _____ (not use) anaesthetics to perform operations.
6 Before iron was invented, soldiers _____ (fight) using bronze swords, but they weren't very strong and often changed shape in battle.
7 The Romans _____ (make) themselves sick, so that they could eat more during their huge banquets.
8 Why _____ people _____ (eat) garlic in Ancient Egypt? It was to cure toothache.

4.3

A Using the words in italics, rewrite the second sentence so it has the same meaning as the first.

1 Let's begin.
   I think we _____should begin_____.
2 I suggest we look at the emails first.
   Why _____?
3 I don't understand.
   I _____ you mean.

4 I agree with that idea.
   It's _____ me.
5 From my point of view, it works very well.
   The way _____ things, it works very well.
6 I agree with what you have just said.
   That's _____ point.

GRAMMAR

5.1 comparatives and superlatives

one-syllable adjectives and two-syllable adjectives ending in -y

adjective	comparative	superlative	notes
cheap fast	cheap**er** fast**er**	**the** cheap**est** **the** fast**est**	+-er/the +-est
easy friendly	eas**ier** friendl**ier**	**the** eas**iest** **the** friendl**iest**	-y changes to -i + -er / the +-est
big	bi**gg**er	**the** bi**gg**est	adjective ending in *CVC double final consonant
large	larg**er**	**the** larg**est**	adjective ending in -e, add -r / the + -st

*CVC – consonant, vowel, consonant

two-syllable and longer adjectives

adjective	comparative	superlative	notes
important	more/less important than	the most/least important	+ more/less … than, or the most/the least … in the …

irregular adjectives

adjective	comparative	superlative
good	better	the best
bad	worse	the worst
Far	further/farther	the furthest/farthest

ways of comparing

Here are some common expressions used for making comparisons: *It's exactly/about the same as …, It's very similar to …, It's not as … as*:

*It's **exactly the same as** the one we had.*
*It's **very similar** to somewhere I stayed.*
*He's **not as tall as** I expected.*

It's a lot/much/far more + adjective:
*It's **far more beautiful** than I imagined.*
It's a little/a little bit/slightly:
*It's **slightly smaller** than the last flat I lived in.*

using superlatives

Here are some common expressions used with superlatives: *by far the most …, one of the most …, the second (third/fourth) most …*

*It's **by far the most** delicious meal I've ever eaten.*
*It's **one of the most** beautiful places in the world.*

We often use superlatives with a phrase beginning *in the …*:

*She's by far the best student **in the class**.*
*It's one of the tallest buildings **in the world**.*

5.2 question tags

To make question tags, add auxiliary verb + pronoun at the end of the question. For a positive sentence, use a negative tag: *You **play** tennis, **don't you**?* For a negative sentence use a positive tag: *They **weren't** here, **were they**?*

Use contractions in the tag, not the full verb: *He's nice, isn't he?* NOT ~~He's nice, is not he?~~ N.B. Use a comma before the question tag and a question mark after it.

	positive verb + negative tag	negative verb + positive tag
present	You're twenty, aren't you?	She doesn't swim, does she?
past	They came back, didn't they?	You didn't see Tim, did you?
present perfect	You've lost it, haven't you?	He hasn't seen us, has he?
future	I'll be back by 10.00, won't I?	We won't lose, will we?

Use question tags to check information that you think is true. Also use question tags to sound less direct (a way to sound polite).

If we are sure of the information, the intonation falls on the question tag:

You're coming tomorrow, aren't you?
(expect the answer 'yes'.)

If we are really not sure, the intonation rises on the question tag:

She's from Europe, isn't she?
(maybe she isn't)

5.3 polite requests

request	responses
Could you carry this bag **for me**? **Could you** bring your laptop with you?	Yes, of course. I'm afraid I can't/ I'm sorry, I can't.
Could you tell me the way to the hotel? **Could you tell me** what time it is?	Yes, I can. It's … Let me have a look.
Do you know what time the shops open? **Do you know** how to get there?	I'm not sure.
Would you mind com**ing** a little bit earlier? **Would you mind** book**ing** us a table?	Of course not. OK/Sure.

watch out!

Could you tell me …? and *Do you know …?* are not direct questions; the word order is the same as for statements:

Could you tell me what time it is?
NOT ~~Could you tell me what time is it?~~

Do you know what time the shops open?
NOT ~~Do you know what time do the shops open?~~

Would you mind … + -ing:

Would you mind watering my plants when I go away?
NOT ~~Would you mind to water …?~~

Would you mind …? is followed by a negative response:

Would you mind helping me? No, of course not.
(I'm happy to help you) NOT ~~Yes, of course.~~
(I would mind helping you = I'm not happy to help you)

PRACTICE

5.1

A Complete the sentences with the comparative or superlative form of the adjectives in brackets.

1 We usually fly to Italy instead of going in the car, because it's _____. (quick)

2 They had to travel _____ than they wanted to find a hotel. (far)

3 When I was a teenager, I was much _____ than I am now. (not confident)

4 He's one of _____ children in the class. (naughty)

5 Exams are much _____ now than they were when I was at school. (easy)

6 Sweden is _____ than Norway. (big)

7 K2 is the second _____ mountain in the world. (high)

8 This book is slightly _____ to understand than his last book. The plot is very complicated. (difficult)

9 He used to be a teacher, but he's decided to become a firefighter. It's a much _____ job. (dangerous)

10 It's by far _____ film I've ever seen. (good)

B Rewrite the sentences using the words in bold, so that they have the same meaning.

1 My brother is slightly taller than I am. **bit**

_____

2 The journey to the coast took much longer than we had expected. **far**

_____

3 It's easily the most expensive restaurant I've ever been to. **by**

_____

4 Your shoes and my shoes are almost the same. **similar**

_____

5 People here are much healthier now that they have clean water. **lot**

_____

5.2

A Match 1–8 with a)–h) to make tag questions.

1 Clive was an engineer,
2 You're from Ethiopia,
3 Shania isn't an actress,
4 They haven't been here before,
5 He'll be home soon,
6 You work here,
7 She hasn't met you,
8 They won't finish on time,

a) have they?
b) won't he?
c) has she?
d) aren't you?
e) is she?
f) will they?
g) wasn't he?
h) don't you?

B Find and correct the mistakes. There is one mistake in each question.

1 You weren't happy, weren't you?
2 It'll probably rain, doesn't it?
3 She researched her roots, didn't her?
4 They always ask tricky questions, they don't?
5 I take after my dad, doesn't he?
6 You've met Kevin's fiancée, have not you?
7 I put my foot in it yesterday, haven't I?
8 My mentor will give me a hand, he won't?
9 You had a lot on your mind, doesn't you?
10 Phil and Luke are on holiday, are not they?

5.3

A Find the mistakes and correct them. There is an extra word or two in each line.

1 A: Excuse me, could you is hold the door for me?
   B: Yes, I do of course.

2 A: Do you know when the next train does to leaves?
   B: I'm not OK sure.

3 A: Would you to mind staying behind after the meeting?
   B: It's sure. That's fine.

4 A: Could is possible you tell me what Tim's phone number is?
   B: Let me have a to look.

5 A: Would you mind to looking after my bag while I go to the bathroom?
   B: No, of course not mind.

6 A: Could you tell for me the way to the station?
   B: Yes, so I can.

VOCABULARY BANK

1 A Complete the family tree with the words in the box.

~~in-laws~~ sister-in-law niece nephew grandparents on my mother's side ex-husband stepfather stepdaughter

B Tell your partner about one or two people in your family.

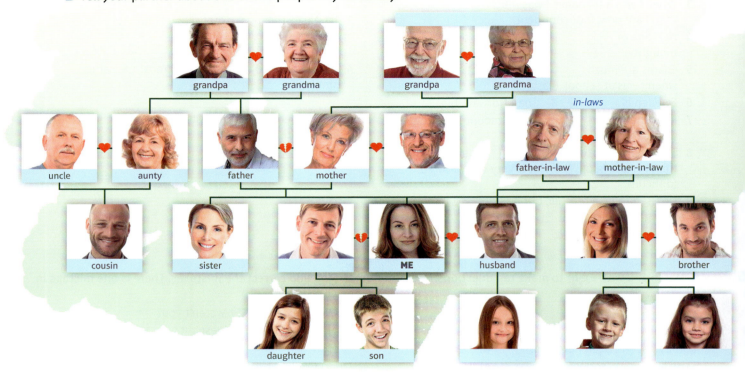

Lesson 1.2 COLLOCATIONS with *take, get, do* and *go*

1 Write the words and phrases in italics in the correct places in the word webs below.

1 *your best, exercise, nothing for you, the cleaning*

do

___*hobby*___ (action)

___*well*___ (good effort)

___*the washing up*___ (something at home)

___*you good*___ (be affected)

3 *a look, the blame, sugar, ages*

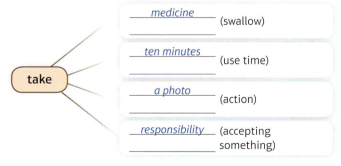

take

___*medicine*___ (swallow)

___*ten minutes*___ (use time)

___*a photo*___ (action)

___*responsibility*___ (accepting something)

2 *fired, a prize, excited, food poisoning*

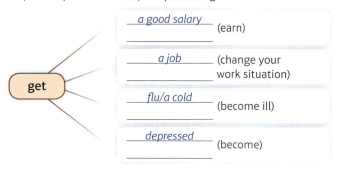

get

___*a good salary*___ (earn)

___*a job*___ (change your work situation)

___*flu/a cold*___ (become ill)

___*depressed*___ (become)

4 *on holiday, crazy, together, badly*

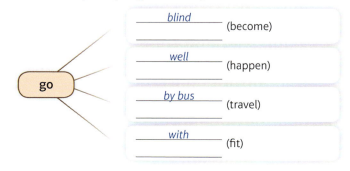

go

___*blind*___ (become)

___*well*___ (happen)

___*by bus*___ (travel)

___*with*___ (fit)

Lesson 2.1 PREPOSITIONS of place

1 Match descriptions 1–5 with pictures A–E.

1 They drove <u>along</u> the motorway, and <u>over</u> the bridge.
2 They went <u>around</u> the city.
3 They drove <u>through</u> the main square, <u>past</u> the post office and turned left <u>by</u> the station.
4 The hotel is <u>near</u> the city centre, <u>between</u> the National Museum and the cathedral.
5 The house is <u>next to</u> the supermarket, <u>opposite</u> the cinema.

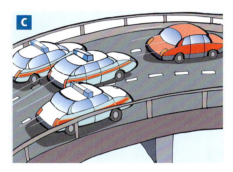

Lesson 2.2 THE NEWS

1 A Read the text and match the words and phrases in bold with definitions 1–10 below.

1 a group of criminals who work together
   _____
2 thieves carrying weapons
   _____ _____
3 an attack by criminals on a bank, shop, etc., to steal money or valuable things _____
4 (doing something) while threatening to shoot someone _____ _____
5 people whose job it is to protect people or a place, or to make sure that a person does not escape _____ _____
6 leave a place or dangerous situation when someone is trying to catch you _____
7 people who saw the crime
   _____ _____
8 took people who were involved in a crime away (to a police station) _____
9 warn people that something bad is happening
   _____ _____ _____
10 made someone do this _____

Two **security guards** were kidnapped and held hostage for twelve hours by a **gang** of **armed robbers**, who attempted to **raid** a security depot. The robbers held the guards **at gunpoint** and **forced** them to hand over keys and security information. They then proceeded to fill a lorry with more than £53 million in notes. Another £150 million was left behind because there was no more room in the getaway vehicle. Luckily, one of the guards managed to **raise the alarm**, and the police arrived and **arrested** the gang before they could **escape**. **Eye witnesses** said that they saw at least eight men being arrested.

B Divide the words and phrases into two groups: people and actions. Which words do not fit in either group?

C Tell your partner about a crime you've heard about. It can be from the news, a film or your own experience.

VOCABULARY BANK

Lesson 3.1 EXPRESSIONS with *get*

1 A Look at the examples for the different uses of *get*.

get + noun = obtain
*Sophie **got a new job** yesterday.*

get + noun = receive
*He **got a letter** from the company.*

get + noun = buy
*Can you remember to **get some milk** on the way home?*

get somewhere
*What time did you **get here**?*

get + adjective
*I'm **getting bored** of this.*

get in phrasal verbs
*I really need to **get on with** my work.*

B Underline the expressions with *get* in sentences 1–6. Match each sentence with the correct use of *get* in Exercise 1A

1 He gets money by selling furniture on the internet.
2 I don't know when I'll get around to finishing that book.
3 We need to get permission to use the room.
4 I'm getting tired. Shall we finish there?
5 Did you manage to get some new trousers?
6 What time does the train get to Budapest?

Lesson 3.2 IDIOMS

1 A Match pictures A–F with the idioms in the box.

be in two minds   let your hair down   break the ice   travel light   learn (something) by heart   go window shopping

B Complete the sentences with the idioms above.

1 Tomorrow there's a test on this poem. I have to _____ it _____ _____.
2 I'm _____ _____ _____. I don't know if I want the black one or the red one.
3 Everyone was nervous, so Jackie told a few jokes to _____ _____ _____.
4 He always _____ _____. He only takes one suitcase even for long trips.
5 I've got no money at the moment but we can go _____ _____ if you want.
6 You've been working non-stop. Why don't you go out and _____ _____ _____ _____?

C What do you think the idioms mean? Use a dictionary to help you.

Lesson 4.1 PERSONAL QUALITIES

1 A Complete the sentences with the adjectives in the box.

> reliable   sensible   easy-going
> aggressive   bright   honest   keen
> punctual   moody   independent

1 She is very _____. She works well by herself.

2 You never know what to expect. She's very _____, so one minute she's happy, and the next minute, she's shouting at you.

3 She's very _____. I'm sure she will know what to do if there's a difficult situation.

4 He's extremely _____. He is never late for appointments.

5 My new manager is very _____. She doesn't mind what time we get to work, what we wear. She never looks stressed.

6 He always tells the truth. He's very _____.

7 She's always looking for extra jobs to do. She's very _____.

8 He's very _____. He learns very quickly.

9 You know that you can trust and depend on him. He's hard-working and very _____.

10 He nearly attacked one of his employees when he arrived late for the meeting. He's very _____.

B Look at the adjectives in the box again. Do they describe positive or negative characteristics? Do you have any of these characteristics?

Lesson 4.1 WORKING LIFE

1 A Match descriptions 1–3 with jobs A–C.

1 I work as a _____ for a large corporation. I usually **work nine-to-five**, but sometimes I have to work late. My job involves checking and responding to emails, **answering phone enquiries** and **organising** my boss's diary.

2 I'm an _____. I tend to **work long hours**. **I'm responsible for** a small team of people. I spend a lot of my time attending meetings, and **dealing with problems**. I **advise clients** on their accounts and **write updates and reports** for the website.

3 I'm a _____. Lots of people wouldn't like what I do, because it's **an outdoor job**, and it's a **physical job**, but I love it. I **work for myself**, so I can be very independent, and I **work flexible hours**, which is good for me. It's a very sociable job, too. I talk to people all day long. I couldn't do **an office job**. I would die of boredom!

Window cleaner

Personal assistant

Accountant

B Work in pairs. What do the phrases in bold mean?

Lesson 4.1 CONFUSING WORDS

1 A Choose the correct option from the words in bold to complete the pairs of sentences.

1 **actually · currently**
   a) I expected the first week in my new job to be awful, but _____ it was fine.
   b) I am _____ working in London, but before I was working in Paris.

2 **career · course**
   a) She's doing a Spanish _____ at the moment, and she's really enjoying it.
   b) Ted spent most of his _____ as a teacher.

3 **borrow · lend**
   a) Do you think you could _____ me a pen?
   b) I had to _____ some money from a friend.

4 **argument · discussion**
   a) We had an interesting _____ about the Prime Minister and we all agreed he should resign.
   b) I had an _____ with my mother. She's always telling me what to do!

5 **miss · lose**
   a) Hurry up, or we'll _____ the bus.
   b) Why do I always _____ my car keys?

B Check your answers in a dictionary.

VOCABULARY BANK

Lesson 5.1 TECHNOLOGY

1 Match words and phrases 1–10 with pictures A–J.

1 plug it in
2 press the button
3 have an injection
4 have an operation
5 run out of petrol
6 break down
7 (not) get a connection
8 restart/reboot the computer
9 do an experiment
10 switch it on/off

A

B

C

D

E

F

G

H

I

J

Lesson 5.2 WORD BUILDING noun (suffixes)

1 A Look at the table in Exercise B. It shows six different suffixes used to form nouns from verbs and adjectives.

B Underline the stressed part of each word in the table. What patterns do you notice about where the stress occurs?

In -ation words, the stress always comes on the a of -ation.

-ation	educa**tion** rela**xa**tion imagina**tion** immi**gra**tion
-ion	pollu**tion** instruc**tion** depres**sion** competi**tion**
-ment	enter**tain**ment im**prove**ment em**ploy**ment a**gree**ment
-ing	**run**ning **smok**ing **laugh**ing **eat**ing
-ness	**weak**ness **lone**liness **happi**ness **kind**ness
-ity	crea**tiv**ity stu**pid**ity sensi**tiv**ity responsi**bil**ity

C Cover the table and complete sentences 1–10 with the correct form of the verbs and adjectives in brackets.

1 I think a bit of _____ (compete) in schools is a good thing.
2 There has been a great _____ (improve) in his work recently.
3 Dealing with problem clients is not my _____ (responsible).
4 _____ (lonely) is one of the worst aspects of getting old.
5 He suffers from _____ (depress).
6 Try to use your _____ (imagine).
7 I couldn't believe my own _____ (stupid)!
8 There is live _____ (entertain) from 8p.m.
9 I was amazed by his _____ (kind).
10 I didn't hear the last _____ (instruct).

pay
imitate
heavy
skate
informal
direct
achieve
quote
dance
fit
promote
secure

2 Change the words above to the correct noun form and add them to the table.

Lesson 1.2

3 C Look at your drawing. Does it include these things?

1 wheels   2 saddle   3 chain   4 handlebar

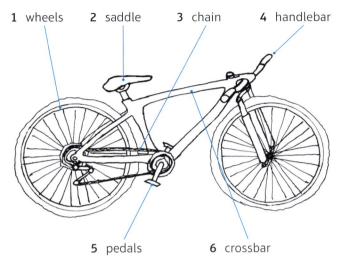

5 pedals   6 crossbar

Lesson 1.2

7 B Read the text and check your answers.

Stella magazine commissioned YouGov, a research agency, to interview over 1,000 women in the UK about everything from their eating habits to their relationships and family values, to find out what they really think. Here are some of the results.

Eighty percent of women say that losing their health is their greatest concern, followed by putting on weight (52%) and losing their jobs (24%). It seems that British women aren't too happy with their bodies: twenty-three percent of women are on a diet now and fifty-eight percent have **gone on a diet** in the past. Only four percent of women **do** more than seven hours' **exercise** per week, while twenty-one percent do no exercise at all.

The biggest challenge for modern women is balancing home and work life (82%), followed by bringing up happy children (56%) and finding time for themselves (52%).

As for their love lives, nine percent of women aged 45–54 met their husbands through the internet, and forty-nine percent of women believe that the best age to **get married** is between 25 and 29.

And what about the relationships between men and women? Fifty-nine percent think fathers should **take more responsibility** for their children. These women are also less than content with their husbands' efforts at home: fifty-one percent say they currently **do** over seventy-five percent of the **housework**. Despite this, over seventy percent of women would prefer to have a male boss than a female.

And their heroes? The woman they most admire is ex-Prime Minister Margaret Thatcher (7%), followed by the Queen (5%).

Lesson 1.3

8 A Student A: read your instructions below.

You work for a famous business school. Student B wants to do a course at the school. Interview him/her. Use the following prompts and ask about:

- his/her reason for doing the course
- his/her work experience
- his/her expectations of the course
- his/her plans for the future

Prepare the questions. Remember to ask your partner why he/she is a good candidate for the school and, at the end, if he/she has any queries about the business school.

B Change roles and role-play the interview again.

Lesson 2.1

1 B Read and check your answers.

HOLLYWOOD versus history

Fact or fiction:

1 Fiction: the film *The Last Samurai* does tell the story of the samurai rebellion, but the character Nathan Algren did not exist.

2 Fiction: in truth, we know very little about William Shakespeare's personal life, or what provided his inspiration.

3 Partly true: the film *Braveheart* does tell the story of how William Wallace fought to free Scotland, but kilts were not worn in Scotland until 300 years later. And there are many other historical inaccuracies.

4 Partly true: the film *Apollo 13* was praised for its accuracy. Much of the dialogue was taken directly from recordings. However, the pilot's exact words were, 'OK, Houston, we've had a problem here'.

Lesson 2.1

8 A Student B: write *Have you ever …?* questions using the prompts in the box below.

win a competition/some money
eat something very unusual
break a bone in your body
lock yourself out of the house
ride a horse/motorbike
climb a mountain/run more than two kilometres

COMMUNICATION BANK

Lesson 2.4

6 B Student A: Look at the picture story. What happened? Why was the robbery attempt a failure? Prepare to tell your story to your partner using the phrases in Exercise 5C.

Lesson 3.3

6 B Change roles and role-play the situation.

Student B

You are a guest at a hotel. Your room is too small. Ten minutes ago you called reception to ask if there are any suites available. Then room service arrived with a trolley of sweets (cakes, ice cream, etc.). Call reception to make your complaint.

Student A

You are a receptionist at a hotel. A guest calls to make a complaint. Start the conversation by saying 'Reception. How can I help you?'

Hello. Yes, I'm afraid I have a problem … Explain the problem again and ask if there is a suite available.

Apologise for the misunderstanding. Explain that there are no suites available at the moment, but there will be tomorrow.

Check details and thank the receptionist for their help.

Confirm details, apologise again and end the call.

Lesson 3.2

7 D Check your answers.

1 False. Compare: *This is absolutely correct.* (formal) *This hits the nail on the head.* (informal)

2 True. The order of the words in *hit the nail on the head, let's face it, close to my heart,* etc. cannot be changed.

3 True. They don't have much time. *They're running out of time.* (present continuous) *We didn't finish. We ran out of time.* (past simple)

4 True. *It's close to my heart* = I feel passionate about it.

Lesson 4.1

A Work out your score. Add up the number of points (0, 1 or 2) for each answer. Use your total to find out if you work like a millionaire.

Question 1	a) 0	b) 1	c) 2
Question 2	a) 1	b) 2	c) 0
Question 3	a) 0	b) 1	c) 2
Question 4	a) 1	b) 2	c) 0
Question 5	a) 0	b) 1	c) 2

re 8–10   You work like a millionaire!

are very ambitious and enjoy your work. going. Sooner or later all your hard work will off and you can live like a millionaire, too.

re 6–7   You have millionaire potential!

understand hard work, and if you make it top priority, you could be a millionaire, too. focused on your goal.

re 0–5   You don't work like a millionaire!

clearest characteristics of self-made onaires is that they work hard and they their work. You seem to prefer a work–life nce, where work and money are not your riorities.

Lesson 4.1

8 B Read the vocabulary notes and check your answers.

remember • remind

If you **remember** something, a fact or event from the past, or something you earlier decided to do, comes back into your mind:
He suddenly remembered he had to go to the bank.

If someone **reminds** you to do something, or something reminds you of something, they make you remember it:
Can you remind me?

forget • leave

If you want to talk about the place where you have left something, use the verb **leave**, not the verb **forget**. Compare:
I've forgotten my book and I've forgotten my keys.
I've left my keys in the car.
Don't say: *I've forgotten my keys in the car.*

listen • hear

If you **hear** something, you know that sound has been made, and can often recognise what it is:
Did you hear that noise?

If you **listen** to something or someone, you pay attention to the words, sounds and music that they are making:
Can you say that again? I'm sorry, I wasn't listening.

fun • funny

Use **fun** to talk about events and activities that are enjoyable, such as games and parties. We can also use it to talk about events that aren't enjoyable.
Being ill on holiday isn't much fun.

Funny is an adjective that describes someone or something that makes you laugh:
Bob's jokes are really funny.

Lesson 2.4

B Student B: Look at the picture story. What happened? Why was the burglary attempt a failure? Prepare to tell your story to your partner using the phrases in Exercise 5C.

Lesson 4.2

11 Choose one of the job advertisements below and write your covering letter.

FASHION DESIGNER WANTED:

We are looking for a graphic designer with a background in the fashion trade. You should have relevant experience and be up-to-date with fashion trends. Strong hand illustration as well as computer design is essential.
Please submit a copy of your CV with relevant samples of work.

TEACHING ASSISTANT, BAHAMAS

Primary school is looking for a teaching assistant to start ASAP. The school is a short walk from the beach. No formal qualifications are necessary; however, a genuine love for the job is required.
Please forward CVs or contact me for further information.

TRAVEL WRITER REQUIRED.

Travel writer wanted to join our small team. The successful applicant will travel around the world, staying in luxury hotels, and dining in fine restaurants. He/She will need to send a weekly update, including a short review. No previous experience required, but good communication skills and a love of travel essential.

Lesson 5.2

1 C Check your answers.

1 Nobody has ever done it, but in theory, yes it is possible.

2 Because it is made of frozen water. It must be below zero degrees Celsius to freeze.

3 Yes. If you travel, you'll notice that you can see different constellations of stars. This is because the surface of the Earth is curved.

4 When we cut an onion, it releases a substance called lachrymatory-factor synthase. When a very small amount goes in your eye it irritates the eye. We then produce tears (we cry) to wash the substance away.

5 Neither hot nor cold. A rainbow is an optical phenomenon caused by the refraction and reflection of sunlight by water. It is the same temperature as the air around it.

6 Because the heavier you are, the more difficult it is to push you out of the ring (which is how you win a sumo wrestling match).

Lesson 1.3

8 A Student B: read your instructions below.

You want to do a course at a famous business school which is well-known for its practical courses. It will give you contacts in the business world. Think about these things:

*   the business you want to start
*   relevant work experience you have with another company

Student A will interview you for the course. He/She will ask about yo

*   reason for doing the course
*   expectations of the course
*   work experience
*   plans for the future

Prepare your answers and think of some questions to ask about the school.

B Change roles and role-play the interview again.

Unit 1 Recording 3

Part one

Is your brain male or female? Well, you might think it's a strange question but some researchers have found that men and women's brains are actually wired differently. So, let's do a test to see if your brain is male or female. In a moment, we're going to ask you to draw a picture of a bicycle. So, make sure you have a pen or pencil ready.

Part two

OK, so I want you to draw a picture of a bicycle. You have exactly one minute, starting now … Make it as beautiful or normal as you like. Include as much detail as you can. You've got forty-five seconds left … You've got another fifteen seconds …
You've got five seconds left … four, three, two, one, zero, stop. Right, stop drawing please. Now, write down on your piece of paper, whether you, the artist, are male or female. That's all we need to know for the experiment. Now turn to page a hundred and fifty-eight to see what a real bike looks like.

(For this edition, turn to page eighty three.)

Unit 1 Recording 4

Part three

Now, count up the parts on your drawing. Did you include wheels? A handlebar? A saddle? A chain? A crossbar? Pedals? Did your bike have at least five parts? And could it work? Now for the difference between the men's drawings of a bicycle and the women's: female drawings often include a person riding the bike; men's drawings don't usually include a person. This is a clear indication that women think people are important. Men, on the other hand, are more interested in getting the machine right. So, how did you do? Is your brain male or female?

Unit 1 Recording 5

Conversation 1

S = student   T = teacher

T: And what about your expectations of the course?
S: Well, as I said, I've studied English for many years and spent time in Britain, but that was a few years ago. So for me the most important thing is to just refresh … and try to remember my English and practise speaking and listening.
T: OK. You've got a very good level of English so we'd put you in the advanced class. Is there anything else?
S: Could I ask a question?
T: Of course.
S: I can take the morning class from nine to twelve. Is that right?
T: Yes, that's right.
S: And in the afternoon there are options? Optional classes?
T: Yes, these are special classes with a special focus like English idioms, conversation, pronunciation. We have the full list here.
S: I see. Thank you.
T: No problem. OK, well, thank you very much.

Conversation 2

I = Interviewer   A = Applicant

I: There are a couple of things I'd like to ask about, Jade. Your CV says you have some experience of looking after children?
A: Yes, I was a tutor on a summer camp last year.
I: Can I ask you about that? What type of things did you do?
A: Um, well, I organised games.
I: Games for?
A: The children.
I: OK. And what age were the children?
A: Um … seven to ten.
I: OK. And you enjoyed it?
A: Yes.

I: What aspect, what part did you enjoy, would you say?
A: I suppose I'd have to say I liked the games best.
I: And any problems?
A: Um, no.
I: What about the different ages? We often find that different ages together can be difficult.
A: It depends. In my opinion, you can usually get the older children to help the younger ones.

Conversation 3

I = Interviewer   S = Student

I: I think that's about it. Do you have any questions? Any queries?
S: Um, yes, actually I do have a query.
I: Yes, go ahead.
S: It's about online classes at the university.
I: Right.
S: If I'm accepted, I saw that there are … urm, that it's possible to take some courses online.
I: That's right.
S: So I wouldn't need to attend classes?
I: Not for the online courses. But, erm … well, one thing I'd like to say is that the online courses are, in many ways, more difficult than face-to-face courses. Certainly in terms of reading and writing, they're really quite demanding.

Unit 1 Recording 7

OK so I'm going to tell you something about myself. My name is Monica Nielson and I live in a small town near Bologna, in Italy. I think three words that describe me would be happy, talkative and hard-working. One of the things I love about my lifestyle is that I love the house where I live. I live in an apartment with my boyfriend, and it's an old apartment in the historical part of town, so it's very beautiful. It's quite small, so I suppose that's one thing I don't like. My favourite smell is the smell of the sea. We live quite far from the sea here, but in the summer, I love to drive to the coast, and breathe the sea air. It makes me feel good. And, finally … if I could change one thing about the past, I would bring my grandmother back. She was a lovely lady and I miss her a lot.

Unit 2 Recording 3

P1 = Presenter 1   P2 = Presenter 2   R = Rosie (a film historian)

P1: Hi and welcome to The Film Show, where today we're looking at the Hollywood biopic and why it's become so popular. Now, Hollywood has always used true stories in its films. In fact, they began making successful films in the 1920s, and since then there have been thousands of films based on true stories.
P2: That's right, but in recent years, there's been more and more biopics. Directors have turned to the lives of famous people as a source of material. So, why is it that some of the best films in recent years have been based on real events, or inspired by real people?
P1: Today, we're talking to Rosie Truman, an actor and a film historian. Rosie, why do you think Hollywood is doing so many biopics?
R: Well, one reason is that audiences really enjoy films about people that they already know something about, but they want to know more. So, from these films we've learnt something. We've learnt about the difficult lives of some of the biggest music legends, like Ray Charles and Johnny Cash. And we've learnt about the lives of politicians, like George Bush, or sporting heroes, like Muhammad Ali. It's a way in which Hollywood can actually teach us about history in an entertaining way. And it's interesting.
P2: Yes, I think that's right.
P2: But what about the actors, Rosie? I mean, many of the actors have won Oscars for their roles in these films. What's it like for them?

R: Well, I think actors just love these roles. It's very exciting to be asked to play a character who everyone already knows. Look at Helen Mirren. She won an Oscar for her role playing the Queen, and it's probably one of her greatest successes.

P1: Oh, absolutely! So, how do they do it? How does an actor prepare for a role like this? Do they meet the person that they're going to play?

R: Well, yes, obviously, if that person is still alive, then that's a great way for the actor to study the character, to see how they move and how they talk. In fact, I know that Helen Mirren met the Queen for tea, you know, very English. And that really helped her to understand her character. And Will Smith, who played Muhammad Ali … well, when they met, they got on really well, and … and they became friends.

P2: But what about playing a character that everyone knows, like George Bush, for example?

R: Yes, it's funny actually, when you're playing a character that people recognise, you have to work really hard at getting the voice right. Josh Brolin played George Bush. And when he was preparing for the film, he talked to himself all day in a Texan accent. He even phoned hotels in Texas, just so he could listen to their accent.

P1: Really? That's funny. What about actors who can't meet the character in person? What do they do?

R: Well, there are other ways to prepare. Audrey Tautou, for example. She played Coco Chanel. So she couldn't meet her in person, but she watched hours and hours of film footage. She watched her in interviews, and she looked at the photographs. Tautou wanted to look like Coco Chanel when she was on screen, so that we would recognise the image.

P2: That's right. And it was a beautiful film.

R: It was, and you know one of the things …

Unit 2 Recording 6

P = Presenter   N1 = 1st news clip   N2 = 2nd news clip
N3 = 3rd news clip   N4 = 4th news clip

P: Hello. I know what I was doing. Do you?

N1: Buckingham Palace has announced the death of Diana, Princess of Wales. The Princess, who was thirty-six, died late last night in a car crash in central Paris.

N2: It's one small step for man, one giant leap for mankind.

N3: Breaking news in here at five live. There are reports that a plane has crashed into the World Trade Center in New York. That's a plane is reportedly crashed into the World Trade Center in New York, setting it on fire …

N4: President Kennedy and Governor John Connally of Texas were shot today from an ambush as President Kennedy's motorcade left the centre of Dallas …

Unit 2 Recording 8

W = Woman   M = Man

M: OK, so, tell me all about it …

W: Well, in the beginning, I was at home, and … um … this was just one morning before a very important interview …

M: Uh-huh.

W: And … um … I didn't feel well, so my mother had given me some pills, and um … then I didn't think anything more about it. So, anyway, erm … I then got on to the tube, um … to go for my interview.

M: Right, and what happened then?

W: Well, um … clearly I must have fallen asleep, because I wasn't feeling great by this time. And um, I'm starting to feel sleepy, so I'm thinking I must have fallen asleep. Anyway, erm … I was getting some funny looks, even before I fell asleep, but anyway. I fell asleep, and then I realised, before long, um … I must have been having a dream, I suppose, about my mother. And all of a sudden, I've woken up, but I haven't just woken up, I've woken up shouting the word, 'Mum!'.

M: No! You're joking!

W: At the top of my voice, in a packed, quiet tube.

M: Oh no!

W: Yes, and everybody's staring at me, and that did not help, er, matters. Anyway, I've got off the tube, and I've then arrived at my interview, put all that behind me, I'm not, I'm still not feeling a hundred per cent perfect, but nevertheless arrived at my interview on time, and go in, and think, actually 'This is going rather well. They're not saying an awful lot, and come to think of it, they're looking at me in a rather strange way.'

M: Right …Then what?

W: Well, the next thing I knew, I have left the interview, and said 'thank you very much for seeing me, blah-di-blah … and gone to the ladies' room. And there in the mirror, I could see what everyone was looking at, and why they couldn't say anything,

M: What was it?

W: My face had swollen up!

M: Ah! No way!

W: It was bright red, and …

M: No!

W: and covered in blotches, spots …

M: Oh! You're kidding!

W: Yes, and the pills that my mother had given me were so out-of-date that they had caused an allergic reaction …

M: Oh! How embarrassing!

W: I know.

Unit 2 Recording 9

M = Man   W2 = 2nd woman   W = Woman

M: OK. What do we reckon? True or false?

W2: Erm … I don't know. I think it might be false because … I don't know …

M: Yeah, she was a little bit slow in telling the story …

W2: I don't know if your mum would give you out-of-date pills …

M: Yeah, would a mother giver her daughter out-of-date pills?

W2: I think false.

M: It sounded like she was trying to think of what to say next, so … you t think false, I think false.

W: Yes, it was false!

Unit 2 Recording 11

OK. This story is about a man called Radu Dogaru, who stole famous paintings from a museum in Rotterdam. In fact, he stole paintings by Picasso, Matisse and Monet. The paintings were worth millions of pounds. What Radu didn't realise was that because the paintings were so famous, he had difficulty selling them. So, he tried to hide them at home. Later, the police thought they had caught Radu. However, the problem was that when they went to search for the paintings, they couldn't find them. It seems that when Radu's mother, Olga, found out what Radu had done, she destroyed the paintings by burning them in her oven in order to protect her son. In the end, Radu was arrested for the theft.

Unit 3 Recording 1

L = Laurie   K = Kenna   J = Javier

L: OK, so what do you think, Kenna? Are you a planner or a procrastinator?

K: Me? Oh a planner, definitely.

L: Yes, I think so. You generally like to do things ahead of time.

K: Absolutely. Yeah. I like to be organised, and know when everything is happening.
I have to be like that, actually. It's the only way to get everything done.

J: Really? I hate planning. I like to leave things until the last minute. I mean, you never know what's going to happen. You might need to change your plans, so why bother making plans in the first place? No, I like not knowing what I'm going to be doing.

K: But that's impossible. What about holidays, for example? You must know what you're doing for your next holiday. I mean, you need to decide where you're going, how you're going to travel, book the dates, get the tickets … There's so much do organise. Surely you have to plan for holidays? You can't just put that off until later.

J: Not really. I don't mind where I go.

K: No, I don't believe, … you're just saying that. I think you do make plans, you just don't like to admit it.

J: No, really. I much prefer to wait and see what happens. I might get invited somewhere.

L: OK, so maybe for holidays. But what about tonight? Have you made any plans for tonight?

K: Yes. Of course. I can tell you exactly what I'm doing tonight. This evening a friend of mine's coming over. We're eating at my house – I'm going to try out a new pasta recipe. And then we're going to the cinema to see that new Argentinian film.

L: Javier?

J: Uhhh … I don't really know. I'll see how I feel. I might go out, or I might just stay at home and relax. I told you. I really don't like to plan.

L: How about at about work? Are you more organised at work? Do you multitask? I mean, how do you make sure you get everything done?

J: … actually, I think I am a procrastinator. I do get jobs done, but I never get started straight away. I tend to waste time and get distracted and leave the job for ages. And then just before the deadline, I work really hard, sometimes all night. And then I don't stop until the job is done. It's quite stressful, but everything gets done in the end.

K: You don't use your time very wisely then? Oh no, I'd hate that. I don't think I could work with you.

Unit 3 Recording 4

Conversation 1

W = Woman   M = Man

W: Hi. Me again. I've sent an attachment with all the figures for the last six months. That should be all you need.

M: Sorry – I didn't catch any of that.

W: I've sent the figures in an attachment. Is that Tom?

M: You've lost me. Who is this?

W: This is Ana Lucia. Is that Tom?

M: No, this is Willy's Burger Bar. What number are you trying to get?

W: 845 6795.

M: I think you've got the wrong number.

W: Oh I'm sorry.

Conversation 2

W = Woman   M = Man

M: I've got a reservation in the name of David Cullinan.

W: Just one moment. Umm, could you repeat the last name?

M: Cullinan. C-u-l-l-i-n-a-n.

W: Cullinan. I can't find the name. Did you make the reservation over the phone?

M: Yes, just yesterday.

W: Sorry, let me just see if there are any messages here. I won't be a moment. I'm sorry. We've got no reservations in the name of Cullinan, and we're fully booked tonight.

M: So you're saying I can't stay here. This is the Sheldon Hotel, yes?

W: No, this is The Felton. With an 'f'.

M: Really? So I'm in the wrong hotel.

W: The Sheldon is on Queen's Road, just around the corner.

M: Oh no. Sorry, can you say that again – where is it?

W: On Queen's Road, just around the corner.

Conversation 3

F = Father   G = Girl

G: You've missed the best bits. You're late.

F: What exactly do you mean? The show starts at 7.00, doesn't it?

G: No, it finishes at 7.00!

F: Didn't you say it starts at 7.00?

G: No, it starts at 5.00 and finishes at 7.00!

F: So what you mean is I've missed the whole show.

G: Yes.

Conversation 4

M = Man   W = Woman

M: We've got nothing for you, I'm afraid.

W: I don't get what you're saying. You're a car rental company, right?

M: Yes, but today's a holiday and all the cars have been booked already.

W: Do you mean to tell me that there's nothing at all? No cars available?

M: There's nothing till tomorrow, I'm afraid.

W: But I definitely booked a car for today, the third of July.

M: It's the fourth of July today. In other words, your booking was for yesterday.

W: It can't be. Is it?

M: It's the fourth today, madam.

W: Oh no, I've got the date wrong.

Unit 3 Recording 7

W = Woman   M = Man

W: OK, so we're looking at creating a video channel.

M: Yep. The first thing, I think, is what's our target audience?

W: Yeah, what's our aim?

M: Well, we came up with this idea.

W: Go on.

M: That it would be really cool to do a series of videos about local places, but with a special angle.

W: Oh that sounds good. What's the angle?

M: An hour to kill. So, say you're in Sydney or Istanbul or anywhere really, and you have an hour to kill, we have a video of someone describing something to do in that place in an hour or less.

W: Oh I see. So the target audience is tourists.

M: It could be tourists or local people. Say you find yourself in a part of the city that you don't know very well.

W: OK.

M: And you have a bit of spare time, by going onto our video channel you get all kinds of suggestions of what to do or where to visit in under an hour. And the clips are filmed on location so you get to see the places, too.

W: I like it. So who will be the presenters? Will you have any star names?

M: No, we don't have any money! We'd get local people to host each video clip, with just one camera, kind of cheap and cheerful, low production values, but really cool content.

W: Who are our competitors or rivals? It must have been done before.

M: Oh I'm sure, but I don't know if it's been done with the angle of an hour to kill.

W: OK. Um, what else? How often will we upload videos?

M: Well we'll try to get coverage of as many cities and towns around the world as possible. So, I don't know, one a day? So in a year we'll have three-hundred-and-sixty-five. Then we just carry on from there.

W: Wow. Very ambitious. What about a name?

M: We thought of One Hour Wonders.

W: One Hour Wonders. I like it!

AUDIO SCRIPTS

Unit 4 Recording 2

Luca

Well, I've always loved sport and swimming. As a kid I used to spend all my free time in the summer on the beach with my friends. We would swim or surf, or just play about in the water. And there was always a lifeguard there on the beach, and I used to think, 'What a **brilliant** job!'. So, when I left school, I trained to be a lifeguard. I really enjoyed the job for a few years. In the summer I would work on the beach, and then in the winter I would go skiing. It was my dream job. I loved it. But after a while, I started to get bored. I was just on this **boiling** beach all day, watching all the **beautiful** people, but I couldn't really enjoy myself, you know. I just had to stand there and watch. So I knew it was time to find something else to do.

Nicola

I used to be an ice-cream taster and for a while it was definitely my dream job. I mean can you imagine anything better than sitting at work eating **delicious** ice cream all day? I was in heaven. I was working for a big company, with a team of food scientists, and our job was to come up with new ideas for ice cream flavours. So, I suppose that was the problem, because a lot of the time, we had to try new flavours, like curry and lime ice cream, or cheese and sausage, and we would have to taste it, and usually it was **terrible**, really disgusting. Now most people would just say, 'Yuck, I'm not eating that again'. But unfortunately, when it's your job, you have to keep tasting it to see if they have made it any better. Sometimes we would taste thirty different ice cream flavours before lunch. So, it wasn't all good.

Amy

I was a professional shopper for a while. It was good fun at first. The lady I worked for was a television presenter, and she needed outfits to wear on television, but she didn't have time to go shopping. So I would go out and buy clothes for her, then she would try them on at home, and I would take back anything that was no good. It was a **fascinating** insight into how some people live. But as time went on I realised she was **impossible** to please. One time I had to buy her an outfit for a special event she was going to, and I bought her a few different things to try on, but she didn't like any of them, and she was really **furious** that I hadn't found her something different. It wasn't really my fault, but I lost my job soon after that.

Unit 4 Recording 5

W1 = Woman 1   W2 = Woman 2   M1 = Man 1   M2 = Man 2

W1: OK, so we're looking at plans for the new café. First of all, we need to decide on the location. Then we'll look at what kind of food we're going to offer, and possible names for the café.
M1: Yes, that sounds good.
W2: OK.
W1: Right. Let's focus on the ideas we had for the location. We looked at some options last time, but we need to make a decision.
M1: I liked the one near the station. It would be really busy during the week when everyone comes in for work. But what does everyone else think?
M2: Yes, I think the station idea is good.
W2: I think we need to decide on the kind of atmosphere we're looking for. The location near the shopping centre would be a really nice place to visit at the weekend.
W1: Hmm.
M1: I'm not sure that I agree, actually. The way I see things, we need to choose the location which will give us the most custom. And I think that will be the café near the station.
M2: And it's cheaper.
W2: That's a good point. I suppose so.
W1: So, shall we say we'll look at the location near the station?
All: Yes. Good idea. Yes, OK.

W1: Good. So, moving on to the next point, what kind of food are we going to serve? What do you think?
M1: Hmm … how about an Italian café?
W2: Mmm … I'm not sure …We talked about Italian, but there are lots of other Italian cafes around. I really feel that it would be hard to make ours different.
W1: OK – good point. I think we should think about something different then. Any ideas?
M2: Well, I was thinking about a Portuguese café, you know, with delicious cakes and pastries. There are quite a lot of Portuguese people in this area, and tourists too. I think that style of café would be really popular.
W2: Yeah, a Portuguese café. I think that's a great idea. What do you think?
All: That's OK. Yeah. Nice.
M1: That's a nice idea. We could do Portuguese-style lunches too, for office workers.
W1: Yes, maybe. So, are we all agreed? A Portuguese café?
All: Yes. That's fine by me.
W1: OK. Let's recap. A Portuguese café selling cakes and lunches, located near the station. Right. So, what would we call it? Café Express?
M1: I'm not sure about that. I think we need to come back to the type of café we're establishing. So Café Portugal? Or something like that …
W2: Why don't we call it Café do Sol? Or Café Lisboa? Café … umm … Café Fado …
W1: I like Café Lisboa. I think it sounds really good and Lisbon's a beautiful city.
M1: Café Lisboa. I like it.
M2: Yes, that sounds good.
W1: OK, we're running out of time. Let's sum up what we've decided. It's going to be a Portuguese café. We think the station location might be good. And we like the name Café Lisboa. Is that right?
All: Yes, I think so. That's right.
W1: OK, so we'll need to decide on …

Unit 4 Recording 8

I'm a pharmacist so I work six days a week. The pharmacy opens at nine a.m., but I need to be at work before then so I can get everything ready. I usually wake up at about six thirty, so I can get the kids up and ready for school, and then go for a run before work. I have to leave home by eight-thirty at the latest. The morning is the busiest time in the pharmacy, so the first thing I do when I get to work is start preparing prescriptions so they're ready for customers to collect. It's a community pharmacy, so I know a lot of the patients quite well. As well as giving out medicines, we try to give advice on healthy living. I think people really appreciate being able to talk to someone in the pharmacy and get advice or treatments without having to see a doctor. I usually have lunch at about one p.m. Sometimes I bring my own lunch, and on other days I like to leave the shop and wander around. I might buy something to eat or even try out a new café. The area near where I work is really nice, and I often bump into people I know. In the afternoon I try to catch up on all the admin tasks that need doing. I check my emails and upload information to our website. I often take phone calls from receptionists, nurses and even doctors from the local surgery, checking information about medication.

I leave the shop at about five thirty p.m. but I usually make some deliveries on my way home. Some of our older patients can't travel to the pharmacy themselves, so they rely on this service. I try to be home by about seven o'clock so that I have time to read to the children and put them to bed. I'm usually too exhausted to do very much in the evening, so I generally just cook supper and watch some television. And then I like to plan my next day in my head before going to bed. It's a long day, but I love my job.

Unit 5 Recording 2

W1 = Woman 1   W2 = Woman 2   M = Man

W1: Why are the windows round on ships?
M: Round windows are stronger, aren't they?
W2: Are they? I've no idea.
W1: That's right. According to the book, they're less likely to break.
W2: Ah.
M: There you go.
W1: What about this second one? How many hairs are there on the human head?
W2: Erm … A million?
M: No, it's not that many, is it?
W2: It depends whose head, doesn't it? On my dad's there are about three.
W1: The answer is about ten thousand.
M: Oh, really?
W2: I think that's a bit of a stupid question because it depends, doesn't it?
M: Well, it was a four-year-old who asked the question.
W2: Oh yeah, that's true.
W1: Next question: What happens when your plane flies over a volcano?
W2: Ummm.
M: Nothing happens, does it? Well, it depends on whether the volcano is erupting? Or whether it's active.
W2: Yeah.
W1: Well, according to the book, Jamieson asked a pilot. And the pilot said as he was flying over the volcano, his engines shut down, stopped working completely.
W2: Scary. Did he get hot?
W1: Hmm, it doesn't say. But he obviously survived. So there you go. Anyway, what about this one? Why did The Beatles break up?
W2: Dunno. They got old, didn't they?
M: No, John Lennon went off with Yoko Ono, didn't he?
W1: Well, Jamieson wrote to Yoko Ono and she replied, 'Because they all grew up, wanted to do things their own way, and they did.'
W2: Oh that's interesting.
M: I'm amazed she replied.
W1: Me, too. OK, last one. After watching a violent video game, the little boy asked why is there war?
W2: Great question.
M: That's a really good question.
W2: Hmm, because men like fighting?
M: Political reasons. One country wants the land or the oil or the gold.
W1: Well, Jamieson asked lots of experts. Most of them didn't or couldn't answer. Then he asked an American army colonel, who said there are four big reasons: different ideologies, a sense of honour, economic reasons, and fear.
M: Uh-huh.
W2: Good question for a four-year-old.
M: And a good answer.

Unit 5 Recording 5

Conversation 1

M = Man   W = Woman

M: Arggh. Oh no.
W: What's the matter?
M: Oh. This cash machine's not working. Do you know if there's another machine somewhere? I really need to get some money.
W: Hmm … I'm not sure. There might be one in the shopping centre.
M: Thanks.

Conversation 2

M = Man   W = Woman

W: Argh!
M: What's the matter?
W: My laptop's just crashed, again. That's the third time it's happened. Would you mind looking at it for me?
M: Sure.
W: Thanks. It's so annoying. I keep losing my documents. Do you know what the problem is?
M: Let me have a look. There's a lot of stuff on here. Why don't you save the documents onto a memory stick?
W: That's a good idea.
M: And then do you want me to try …

Conversation 3

M = Man   W = Woman

W: Customer services. Good morning.
M: Um, yes. I've got a problem with my vacuum cleaner.
W: Could you tell me what the problem is, sir?
M: Yes, I can. It keeps making a funny noise. And it's just not working properly.
W: You say it keeps making a funny noise …
M: Yes, that's right.
W: OK. Let's see if I can find someone who can help you. Could you hold the line, please?
M: Yes, of course.

Conversation 4

M = Man   W = Woman

M: Oh. I don't believe it! Excuse me, this machine's not working. It's just taken my money. Could you give me a refund?
W: I'm afraid I can't do that.
M: Why not?
W: Well, I'm not allowed to give refunds.
M: But I've just lost my money. And I still need a ticket.
W: I can sell you a ticket, but I can't give you a refund.
M: Well, could you tell me who I should speak to?
W: Yes, of course. You need to speak to the manager.
M: OK. Would you mind calling him for me?
W: Of course not. I'll just call him.

Unit 5 Recording 8

I'm going to tell you about Robo-Chef. Basically, Robo-Chef can prepare and cook all your favourite recipes. It works like this. First of all, it washes and prepares all the vegetables, then it prepares your dish, and cooks it for you on your cooker. Robo-Chef comes complete with hundreds of menus already programmed. But you can also programme Robo-Chef with your own recipes, or, if you want to try something new, you can download new recipes whenever you like. All you have to do is choose the dish you want, decide how many people you want Robo-Chef to cook for, and what time you want the meal to be ready. So, let's say you would like a vegetable lasagne for six people, ready by eight o'clock. Then, just make sure you have all the ingredients in the kitchen, press the button, and that's it. You can go out to work, and when you come home in the evening, your delicious supper will be ready. What could be easier? Robo-Chef is the chef of the future.